THE HIERARCHY OF MINDS

THE MIND LEVELS

Selections from the Works of
Sri Aurobindo and The Mother

by Jyoti and Prem Sobel

Sri Aurobindo Ashram
Puducherry, India

First Edition, 1984
Revised Edition 2007

ISBN 978-81-7058-870-2
@Sri Aurobindo Ashram Trust 1984, 2007
Published by Sri Aurobindo Ashram Publication Department
Puducherry – 605 002
Website: http://www.sabda.in
Printed at Sri Aurobindo Ashram Press, Puducherry
PRINTED IN INDIA

Dedicated to

Sri Aurobindo and the Mother
and
all seekers of Truth

SRI AUROBINDO

CONTENTS OVERVIEW

Editor's Note	i
Our godhead calls us	3
Consciousness	5
Mind	13
The Minds of Man	43
The Physical Mind	49
The Vital Mind	61
The Mental Mind	81
The Psychic Mind	105
The Spiritual Mind	123
Towards Supermind	143
Beyond Mind: the Supermind	183
Appendix	197
Glossary	211
References	223

CONTENTS

Editor's Note   i
Our godhead calls us (poem)   1

Consciousness
The secret of consciousness	5
Consciousness as Mind	6
Evolution [1] (poem)	7
Man has to look below the surface	8
The problem of consciousness	8
Consciousness, lila and mind	9

Mind
What is mind?	13
Mind is an inferior power of Supermind	14
The power of consciousness of mind	15
The one self and mind	16
Several capital and common errors about mind	17
The Hidden Plan (poem)	19
The Infinite Adventure (poem)	20
The soul in mind	21
Mind, surface mind and embodied mind	21
The Inconscient (poem)	24
The Dumb Inconscient (poem)	25
The Conscious Inconscient (poem)	26
Mind or active consciousness	27
Liberation of mind	27
The mind of man and the Absolute	29
Mind, Force and Consciousness	30
The transformation of the human mentality	31
Mind in the process of divine knowledge	33

Mind in the higher realisation	34
Evolution [2] (poem)	36
Mind is not the last possibility of consciousness	37
Mind is not sufficient to explain existence	38
Mind and the inner being	39

The Minds of Man
Man, the Thinking Animal (poem)	43
Classification	46
The mixture of the minds	46

The Physical Mind
The physical mind	49
At the outset man lives in his physical mind	49
The stand of the physical mind	50
Response of the physical mind	51
The limitations of the physical mind	51
The physical mind and work	52
The action of the physical mind	53
The physical mind has first to open	53
Change in the physical mind	54
The surface mind	55
The place of the sense-mind	56
The sense-mind (Manas)	57
The sense-mind and the powers of mind	58
Purification of the function of the sense-mind	59
The proper function of the sense-mind	60

The Vital Mind
The vital mind as part of the nature	61
Life (poem)	63
Four parts of the vital being	65

The true vital being	65
The vital mind as part of the vital being	66
The vital mind proper	66
The emotional mind	68
Purification of the vital mind	68
"For man's mind is the dupe of his animal self" (poem)	70
Vital mind as an instrument of desire	71
The rejection of the desire-mind	72
The vital mind, duality and the psychic being	73
Inner experience: the aesthetic mind	76
The vital mind and evolution	76
Release from the desire-mind and the emotional mind	77
The vital mind can be a great force	78
Bride of the Fire (poem)	80

The Mental Mind

Mind and mentalisation	81
The thought-mind	81
The sensational thought-mind	82
Pure intellectual understanding	83
Understanding in the consciousness	84
Separation of the thinker and the thinking	84
Not mental control but control by the Divine Power	86
The original action of the thought-mind	87
Mind also is a half-light	87
Right thought	88
"Mind is a delusion" (poem)	90
The ego-mind	91
Our mind is a house haunted by the slain past (poem)	93

Contents xi

Our real self	94
Essential mentality is idealistic	95
This witness hush is the Thinker's secret base (poem)	96
Silence and the knowledge of the Self	97
Constant silence of the mind	97
The mind has to be quiet during an experience	98
The spectator and creator Mind (poem)	100
Knowledge is not wisdom (poem)	101
Rightly to know and express the Highest	102
The final realisation	103

The Psychic Mind

The word psychic	105
Psychic mind and mental psychic	106
Nature of the psychic	107
The mind and the psychic being	108
Soul and psychic being	109
The inner consciousness and the psychic being	111
The psychic in little children	112
The right object of education	113
The psychic is the solution	114
The psychic and the other parts of the being	115
Identification of the soul with mind	116
Emergence of the soul as distinct from mind	118
Self-consecration from the mind to the inner being	120
Thoughts of the outer mind and psychic thoughts	121
Psychic growth and usefulness of mind	122

The Spiritual Mind

The spiritual mind	123
Spirituality and mind	123
Spirituality helps mind but cannot bring about transformation	124
The spiritual being can develop in mind the higher states of being	126
The first approach of mind to spirit	127
Spirit, Matter and Mind	128
Mind as a derivation from the fullness of self	129
The achievement of the spiritual mind in man	130
The lines of achievement of the spiritual mind	132
The spiritual man's mind	132
The tendency of the spiritualised mind is to go upwards	133
The ascension of Mind	134
"Beyond the spiritual mind" (poem)	136
From the spiritualised mind to Supermind	137
Gradations of Manifestation	138

Towards Supermind

The Kingdom Within (poem)	143
Man's rise to the Infinite	144
Human mind reaches beyond itself	145
Spirit, Atman and Jivatman	147
The widening into the inner mind	150
The inner mind	151
Inner mind and poetic vision	151
The higher mind	152
The higher mind is more powerful than reason	153
Aspects of the higher mind: cognition and will	154
The formation of a luminous mind	156

Contents

The Illumined Mind	157
Poetry of the illumined mind and intuition	160
Intuitive mind or intuitive reason	160
The intuitive mentality is still mind and not gnosis	161
The way to the intuitive mind	162
The intuitive mind	164
The difference between ordinary mind and intuitive mind	165
Poetry of the intuitive mind	166
The Overmind is a delegate of the Supermind Consciousness	168
The cosmic Mind	170
The Cosmic Spirit (poem)	171
Opening to the cosmic mind	172
The nature of the action of the cosmic Mind	173
The universal Mind	174
The ranges above Mind in universal Mind	175
The universal Mind around us	176
The working of the forces of the universal mind	176
How thoughts are created by the forces of the universal mind	177

Beyond Mind: the Supermind

Supermind is beyond mind, life and Matter	183
Transformation (poem)	184
The mind of Light	185
Supermind is Truth-Consciousness	186
The forerunners of a divine multitude (poem)	188
Supermind: the experience of the supreme Infinite	190
To become the divine superman	191

Appendix
  The Various Minds in *Savitri*   197
  How to Think   206

Glossary   211

References   223

EDITOR'S NOTE

Throughout his writings Sri Aurobindo has spoken at length about the five minds of man and the corresponding minds in the universe. The complex terminology he has used illumines their many facets as light illumines a prism.

At a time when humanity is becoming acutely aware that mind cannot solve the problems mind has created, and the reign of *homo sapiens* is over, the first edition of this selection (first published in 1984 and reprinted five times), needed to be revised and enlarged.

This second edition, however, like the first, remain deliberately selective, without omitting any important aspect of each mind level. About fifteen new passages have been added: several conversations of the Mother during the 1950s, some prose writings by Sri Aurobindo and an extract from his poem *Savitri*.

The poems in this compilation, introduced as a complement to the texts in prose, have also been included, not only for their beauty, but as an attempt to be faithful to Sri Aurobindo's unity of expression and of his vision of the future of humanity.

The titles given to each section and each text are ours; in most cases they are taken from Sri Aurobindo's own terminology. The phrase "mental mind" is used by the Mother in her classification.

My gratitude goes to the late Norman Dowsett, to Prem Sobel and Smita Cochet. Their guidance, support and pertinent criticism were a great help in preparing the first edition.

My gratitude also goes to Bob Zwicker, of the Ashram Archives and Research Library, for taking the trouble to take a look at this revised edition, to my good friend and patient Auroville proofreader, Kathryn, and to the Sri Aurobindo Ashram Copyright Department, which has kindly given permission to publish these texts.

Jyoti Sobel
Auroville

CONSCIOUSNESS

Our godhead calls us

Our godhead calls us in unrealised things.
　　Asleep in the wide fields of destiny,
A world guarded by Silence' rustling wings
　　Sheltered their fine impossibility.

But part, but quiver the cerulean gates,
　　Close splendours look into our dreaming eyes,
We bear proud deities and magnificent fates;
　　Faces and hands come near from Paradise.

What shone thus far above is here in us;
　　Bliss unattained our future's birthright is;
Beauty of our dim soul is amorous;
　　We are the heirs of infinite widenesses.

The impossible is the hint of what shall be,
　　Mortal the door to immortality.[1]

　　　　　　　　　　　　　　Sri Aurobindo

CONSCIOUSNESS

The secret of consciousness

There are two states of being, two levels or limits between which all existence stands or moves, a highest limit of supreme consciousness, an omniscient Superconscient, a nethermost limit of supreme unconsciousness, an omnipotent Inconscience. The secret of consciousness reveals itself only when we perceive these two limits and the movement between them which we call the universe.

There can be no consciousness without existence, for the consciousness of a void or a Nihil is a vain imagination, a thing impossible. For Nothing cannot be conscious of anything – cannot be conscious of itself; if it were conscious of itself, it would at once be an existence aware of itself, it would cease to be a Nihil; it would at once be evident that it was all the time an Existence appearing to be Nihil, that it was being or a Being unconscious, but now grown conscious of its own existence. A void, conscious of itself is conceivable, but it would be a void existence and not Nihil. There might be an eternal Non-Being, but that too could not be Nihil; eventually it could only be a supreme superconscient existence exceeding our notion of being. A true Nihil would necessarily be as incapable of consciousness as of existence; out of it nothing could come as in it nothing could be, neiher spirit nor soul nor mind nor Matter.

We have then at one end of things a supreme superconscient existence and a supreme inconscient existence and between them we have consciousness in the universe; but both are two states of one being; what is between also is movement of that one Being between its two ends, its two highest and lowest levels of self-manifestation, *Ekam evadvitiyam*.[2]

Sri Aurobindo

Consciousness as Mind

In man the energising Consciousness appears as Mind more clearly aware of itself and things; this is still a partial and limited, not an integral power of itself, but a first conceptive potentiality and promise of integral emergence is visible. That integral emergence is the goal of evolving Nature.

Man is there to affirm himself in the universe, that is his first business, but also to evolve and finally to exceed himself; he has to enlarge his partial being into a complete being, his partial consciousness into an integral consciousness; he has to achieve mastery of his environment but also world-union and world-harmony; he has to realise his individuality but also to enlarge it into a cosmic self and a universal and spiritual delight of existence.[3]

Sri Aurobindo

Evolution [1]

All is not finished in the Unseen's decree!
    A mind beyond our mind demands our ken;
A life of unimagined harmony
    Awaits, concealed, the grasp of unborn men.

The crude beginnings of the lifeless earth
    And mindless stirrings of the plant and tree
Prepared our thought; thought for the godlike birth
    Broadens the mould of our mortality,

A might no human will or force could gain,
    A knowledge seated in eternity,
A joy* beyond our struggle and our pain
    Is this earth-hampered creature's destiny.

O Thou who climbedst to mind from the dull stone,
Turn to the miracled summits yet unwon.[4]

                                        Sri Aurobindo

---

* Bliss

Man has to look below the surface

A time must come when man has to look below the obscure surface of his egoistic being and attempt to know himself; he must set out to find the real man: without that he would be stopping short at Nature's primary education and never go on to her deeper and larger teachings; however great his practical knowledge and efficiency, he would be only a little higher than the animals. First, he has to turn his eyes upon his own psychology and distinguish its natural elements, – ego, mind and its instruments, life, body, – until he discovers that his whole existence stands in need of an explanation other than the working of the natural elements and of a goal for its activities other than an egoistic self-affirmation and satisfaction.[5]

Sri Aurobindo

The problem of consciousness

The problem of consciousness can only be solved if we go back to a radical state of our existence in which things get back to their reality. For there they are no longer a mass of phenomena which have to be cleared up, classified, organised by the perceptions, conceptions and relative logic of the human intellect. These perceptions, these concepts, this logic belong to an imperfect instrument and the arrangements they make can only be provisional and, at that, one-sided and only half-true or a good deal less than half-true – and even that truth is of an inferior kind, a constructed representation and not truth itself in its own nature. In fact the intellect sees only the phenomenon, it cannot go back behind it; when it tries, it only arrives at other and more occult phenomena. The truth of things can only be perceived when one gets to what may be called summarily the spiritual vision of things and even there completely only when there is not only vision but direct experience in the very substance of one's own being and all being.[6]

Sri Aurobindo

Consciousness, lila and mind

What we see in and around us is a play of God, a "Lila". It is a scene arranged, a drama played by the One Person with his own multitudinous personalities in his own impersonal existence, – a game, a plan worked out in the vast and plastic substance of his own world-being. He plays with the powers and forces of his Nature a game of emergence from the inconscient Self out of which all here began, through the mixed and imperfect consciousness which is all we have now reached, towards a supreme consciousness, a divine nature.

This we cannot now know; our eyes are fixed on a partial outer manifestation which we see and call the universe – though even now we see and know very little of it or about it, – know perhaps a few of its processes but nothing fundamental, nothing of its reality, – and an inner partial manifestation which we do not see but experience and feel and call ourselves. Our mind is shut up in a cleft between these two fragments and tends to regard it as the whole of things and the only tangible and real existence.

It is so that the frog regards himself and his well. But we have to grow out of this frog consciousness and exceed the limits of this well. In the end we come to perceive that we have a truer and divine being of which our petty personality is only a surface and corrupt output, a truer and divine Consciousness in which we must become self-aware and world-aware discarding our present fragmentary and bounded mental vision of self and things.

The term of our destiny is already known to us; we have to grow from what we are into a more luminous existence, from pleasure and pain into a purer and vaster and deeper bliss, from our struggling knowledge and ignorance into a spontaneous and boundless light of consciousness, from our fumbling strength and weakness into a sure and all-understanding Power, from division and ego into universality and unity. There is an evolution and we have to complete it; a human animality or an animal humanity is not enough. We must pass from the inadequate figure of humanity into a figure of the Godhead, from mind to supermind, from the consciousness of the finite to the consciousness of the Infinite, from Nature into Supernature.[7]

Sri Aurobindo

MIND

MIND

What is mind?

Mind, first, the chained and hampered sovereign of our human living. Mind in its essence is a consciousness which measures, limits, cuts out forms of things from the indivisible whole and contains them as if each were a separate integer. Even with what exists only as obvious parts and fractions, Mind establishes this fiction of its ordinary commerce that they are things with which it can deal separately and not merely as aspects of a whole. For, even when it knows that they are not things in themselves, it is obliged to deal with them as if they were things in themselves; otherwise it could not subject them to its own characteristic activity. It is this essential characteristic of Mind which conditions the workings of all its operative powers, whether conception, perception, sensation or the dealings of creative thought. It conceives, perceives, senses things as if rigidly cut out from a background or a mass and employs them as fixed units of the material given to it for creation or possession. All its action and enjoyment deal thus with wholes that form part of a greater whole, and these subordinate wholes again are broken up into parts which are also treated as wholes for the particular purposes they serve. Mind may divide, multiply, add, subtract, but it cannot get beyond the limits of this mathematics. If it goes beyond and tries to conceive a real whole, it loses itself in a foreign element; it falls from its own firm ground into the ocean of the intangible, into the abysms of the infinite where it can neither perceive, conceive, sense nor deal with its subject for creation and enjoyment. For if Mind appears sometimes to conceive, to perceive, to sense or to enjoy with possession the infinite, it is only in seeming and always in a figure of the infinite. What it does thus vaguely possess is simply a formless Vast and not the real spaceless infinite. The moment it tries to deal with that, to possess it, at once the inalienable tendency to delimitation comes in and the Mind finds itself again handling images, forms and words. Mind cannot possess the infinite, it can only suffer it or be possessed by it; it can only lie blissfully helpless under the luminous shadow of the Real cast down on it from planes of existence beyond its reach. The possession of the infinite cannot come except by an ascent to those supramental planes, nor the knowledge of it except by an inert submission of Mind to the descending messages of the Truth-Conscious Reality.[8]

Sri Aurobindo

Mind is an inferior power of Supermind

We know also that Mind is an inferior power of the original conscious Knowledge or Supermind, a power to which Life acts as an instrumental energy; for, descending through Supermind, Consciousness or Chit represents itself as Mind, Force of consciousness or Tapas represents itself as Life. Mind, by its separation from its own higher reality in Supermind, gives Life the appearance of division and, by its farther involution in its own Life-Force, becomes subconscious in Life and thus gives the outward appearance of an inconscient force to its material workings. Therefore, the inconscience, the inertia, the atomic disaggregation of Matter must have their source in this all-dividing and self-involving action of Mind by which our universe came into being. As Mind is only a final action of Supermind in the descent towards creation and Life an action of Conscious-

Mind

Force working in the conditions of the Ignorance created by this descent of Mind, so Matter, as we know it, is only the final form taken by conscious-being as the result of that working. Matter is substance of the one Conscious-Being phenomenally divided within itself by the action of a universal Mind,* – a division which the individual mind repeats and dwells in, but which does not abrogate or at all diminish the unity of Spirit or the unity of Energy or the real unity of Matter.[9]

Sri Aurobindo

The power of consciousness of mind

Mind, as we know it, has a power of consciousness quite distinct from Supermind, no longer a power devolved from it, connected with it and dependent upon it, but practically divorced from its luminous origin, is marked by several characteristics which we conceive to be the very signs of its nature: but some of these belong to Supermind also and the difference is in the way and scope of their action, not in their stuff or in their principle. The difference is that mind is not a power of whole knowledge and only when it begins to pass beyond itself, a power of direct knowledge: it receives rays of the truth but does not live in the sun: it sees as through glasses and its knowledge is coloured by its instruments, it cannot see with the naked eye or look straight at the sun.... It is a power for creation, but either tentative and uncertain and succeeding by good chance or the favour of circumstance or

---

* Mind is here in its widest sense including the operation of an Overmind power which is nearest to the supramental Truth-consciousness and which is the first fountain of the creation of the Ignorance.

else, if assured by some force of practical ability or genius, subject to flaw or pent within unescapable limits. Its highest knowledge is often abstract, lacking in a concrete grasp; it has to use expedients and unsure means of arrival, to rely upon reasoning, argumentation and debate, inferences, divinations, set methods of inductive or deductive logic, succeeding only if it is given correct and complete data and even then liable to reach on the same date different results and varying consequences; it has to use means and accept results of a method which is hazardous even when making a claim to certitude and of which there would be no need if it had a direct or a supra-intellectual knowledge.... All this is the very nature of our terrestrial ignorance and its shadow hangs on even to the thought and vision of the sage and the seer and can be escaped only if the principle of a truth-conscious supramental knowledge descends and takes up the governance of the earth-nature.[10]

Sri Aurobindo

The one self and mind

This the self of man, since it is the essentiality of a mental being, will do through the mind. In the gods the transfiguration is effected by the Superconscient itself visiting their substance and opening their vision with its flashes until it has transformed them; but the mind is capable of another action which is only apparently movement of mind, but really the movement of the self towards its own reality. The mind seems to go to That, to attain to it; it is lifted out of itself into something beyond and although it falls back, still by the mind the will of knowledge in the mental thought continually and at last continuously remembers that into which it has entered. On this the Self through the mind seizes and repeatedly dwells and so doing it is finally caught up into it and at last able to dwell securely in that transcendence. It transcends the mind, it transcends its own mental individualisation of the being, that which it now knows as itself; it ascends and takes foundation in the Self of all and in the status of self-joyous infinity, which is the supreme manifestation of the Self. This is the transcendent immortality, this is the spiritual existence which the Upanishads declare to be the goal of man and by which we pass out of the mortal state into the heaven of the Spirit.[11]

Sri Aurobindo

Several capital and common errors about mind

1. That mind and spirit are the same thing.
2. That all consciousness can be spoken of as "mind".
3. That all consciousness therefore is of a spiritual substance.
4. That the body is merely Matter, not conscious, therefore something quite different from the spiritual part of the nature.

First, the spirit and the mind are two different things and should not be confused together. The mind is an instrumental entity or instrumental consciousness whose function is to think and perceive – the spirit is an essential entity or consciousness which does not need to think or perceive either in the mental or the sensory way, because whatever knowledge it has is direct or essential knowledge, *svayamprakāśa*.

Next, it follows that all consciousness is not necessarily of a spiritual make and it need not be true and is not true that the thing commanding and the thing commanded are the same, are not at all different, are of the same substance and therefore are bound or at least ought to agree together.

Third, it is not even true that it is the mind which is commanding the mind and finds itself disobeyed by itself. First, there are many parts of the mind, each a force in itself with its formations, functionings, interests, and they may not agree. One part of the mind may be spiritually influenced and like to think of the Divine and obey the spiritual impulse, another part may be rational or scientific or literary and prefer to follow the formations, beliefs or doubts, mental preferences and interests which are in conformity with its education and its nature.[12]

Sri Aurobindo

The Hidden Plan

However long Night's hour, I will not dream
    That the small ego and the person's mask
Are all that God reveals in our life-scheme,
    The last result of Nature's cosmic task.
A greater Presence in her bosom works;
    Long it prepares its far epiphany:
Even in the stone and beast the godhead lurks,
    A bright Persona of eternity.
It shall burst out from the limit traced by Mind
    And make a witness of the prescient heart;
It shall reveal even in this inert blind
    Nature, long veiled in each inconscient part,
Fulfilling the occult magnificent plan,
    The world-wide and immortal spirit in man.[13]

                                      Sri Aurobindo

The Infinite Adventure

On the waters of a nameless Infinite
    My skiff is launched; I have left the human shore.
    All fades behind me and I see before
The unknown abyss and one pale pointing light.
An unseen Hand controls my rudder. Night
    Walls up the sea in a black corridor, –
    An inconscient Hunter's lion plaint and roar
Or the ocean sleep of a dead Eremite

I feel the greatness of the Power I seek
    Surround me, below me are its* giant deeps.
    Beyond, the invisible height no soul has trod.
I shall be merged in the Lonely and Unique
    And wake into a sudden blaze of God,
        The marvel and rapture of the Apocalypse.[14]

                              Sri Aurobindo

---

* the.

The soul in mind

To the Life-Spirit, therefore, the individual in whom its potentialities centre is pre-eminently Man, the Purusha. It is the Son of Man who is supremely capable of incarnating God. This Man is the Manu, the thinker, the Manomaya Purusha, mental person or soul in mind of the ancient sages. No mere superior mammal is he, but a conceptive soul basing itself on the animal body in Matter. He is conscious Name or Numen accepting and utilising form as a medium through which Person can deal with substance. The animal life emerging out of Matter is only the inferior term of his existence. The life of thought, feeling, will, conscious impulsion, that which we name in its totality Mind, that which strives to seize upon Matter and its vital energies and subject them to the law of its own progressive transformation, is the middle term in which he takes his effectual station. But there is equally a supreme term which Mind in man searches after so that having found he may affirm it in his mental and bodily existence. This practical affirmation of something essentially superior to his present self is the basis of the divine life in the human being.[15]

Sri Aurobindo

Mind, surface mind and embodied mind

Mind was called by Indian psychologists the eleventh and ranks as the supreme sense. In the ancient arrangement of the senses, five of knowledge and five of action, it was the sixth of the organs of knowledge and at the same time the sixth of the organs of action. It is a common-place of psychology that the effective functioning of the senses of knowledge is inoperative without the assistance of the mind; the eye may see, the ear may hear, all the sense may act, but if the mind pays no attention, the man has not heard, seen, felt, touched or tasted. Similarly, according to psychology, the organs of action act only by the force of the mind operating as will or, physiologically, by the reactive nervous force from the brain which must be according to materialistic notions the true self and essence of all will. In any case, the senses or all senses, if there are other than the ten, – according to a text in the Upanishad* there should be at least fourteen, seven and seven, all senses appear to be only organisations, functionings, instrumentations of the mind-consciousness, devices which it has formed in the course of its evolution in living Matter.

Modern psychology has extended our knowledge and has admitted us to a truth which the ancients already knew but expressed in other language. We know now or we rediscover the truth that the conscious operation of mind is only a surface action. There is a much vaster and more potent subconscious mind which loses nothing of what the senses bring to it; it keeps all is wealth in an inexhaustible store of memory, *akṣitam śravaḥ*. The surface mind may pay no attention, still the subconscious mind attends, receives, treasures up with an infallible accuracy....

Similarly we know that a large part of our physical action is instinctive and directed not by the surface but by the subconscious mind. And we know now that it is a mind that acts and not merely an ignorant nervous reaction from the brute physical brain.

... [This] point(s) to truths which western psychology,

---

* Sri Aurobindo refers to an Upanishad he has not translated. – Ed.

harmpered by past ignorance posing as scientific orthodoxy, still ignores or refuses to acknowledge. The Upanishads declare that the Mind in us is infinite; it knows not only what has been seen but what has not been seen, not only what has been heard but what has not been heard, not only what has been discriminated by the thought but what has not been discriminated by the thought. Let us say, then, in the tongue of our modern knowledge that the surface man in us is limited by his physical experiences; he knows only what his nervous life in the body brings to his embodied mind; and even of those bringings he knows, he can retain and utilise only so much as his surface mind-sense attends to and consciously remembers; but there is a larger subliminal consciousness within him which is not thus limited. That consciousness senses what has not been sensed by the surface mind and its organs and knows what the surface mind has not learned by its acquisitive thought.[16]

Sri Aurobindo

The Inconscient

Out of a seeming void and dark-winged sleep
   Of dim inconscient infinity
A Power arose from the insentient deep,
   A flame-whirl of magician Energy.

Some huge somnambulist Intelligence
   Devising without thought process and plan
Arrayed the burning stars' magnificence,
   The living bodies of beasts and the brain of man.

What stark Necessity or ordered Chance
   Because alive to know the cosmic whole?
What magic of numbers, what mechanic dance
   Developed consciousness, assumed a soul?

The darkness was the Omnipotent's abode,
Hood of omniscience, a blind mask of God.[17]

Sri Aurobindo

The Dumb Inconscient

The dumb Inconscient drew life's stumbling maze;
  A night of all things, packed and infinite,
It made our consciousness a torch that plays
  Between the abyss* and a supernal Light;

It framed** our mind a lens of segment sight,
  Piecing out inch by inch the world's huge mass,
And reason a small hard theodolite
  Measuring unreally the measureless ways.

Yet is the dark Inconscient whence come all,
  The self-same Power that shines on high unwon;
Our night shall be a sky purpureal,
  The torch transmute to a vast godhead's sun.

Man is a narrow bridge, a call that grows,
His soul the dim bud of God's flaming rose.[18]

                              Sri Aurobindo

---

* Its night.
** Made.

The Conscious Inconscient

Because Thou hadst all eternity to amuse,
  O dramatist of death and life and birth,
  O sculptor of the living shapes of earth,
World-artist revelling in forms and hues,

A mathematician Mind that never errs,
  Thou hast played with theorems, numbers, measures, cubes,
  Passed cells, electrons, molecules through Thy tubes,
World-forces for Thy Science's ministers,

And made a universe of Thy theories,
  Craftsman minute, an architect of might.
  Protean is Thy Spirit of Delight,
An adept of a thousand mysteries

Or built some deep Necessity, not Thy whim,
Fate and Inconscience and the snare of Time?[19]

Sri Aurobindo

Mind or active consciousness

Mind, in fact, or active consciousness generally has four necessary functions which are indispensable to it wherever and however it may act and of which the Upanishads speak in the four terms, *vijñāna, prajñāna, saṁjñāna* and *ājñāna*. Vijnana is the original comprehensive consciousness which holds an image of things in its essence, its totality and its parts and properties; it is the original, spontaneous, true and complete view of it which belongs properly to the supermind and of which mind has only a shadow in the highest operation of the comprehensive intellect. Prajnana is the consciousness which holds an image of things before it as an object with which it has to enter into relations and to possess by apprehension and analytic and synthetic cognition. Sanjnana is the contact of consciousness with an image of things by which there is a sensible possession of it in its substance; if Prajana can be described as the outgoing of apprehensive consciousness to possess its object in conscious energy, to know it, Sanjana can be described as the inbringing movement of apprehensive consciousness which draws the object placed before it back to itself so as to possess it in conscious substance, to feel it. Ajnana is the operation by which consciousness dwells on an image of things so as to hold, govern and possess it in power. These four, therefore, are the basis of all conscious action.[20]

Sri Aurobindo

Liberation of mind

From this nature of mental and sense knowledge as it is at present organised in us, it follows that there is no inevitable necessity in our existing limitations. They are the result of an evolution in which mind has accustomed itself to depend upon certain physiological functionings and their reactions as its normal means of entering into relation with the material universe. Therefore, although it is the rule that when we seek to become aware of the external world, we have to do so indirectly through the sense-organs and can experience only so much of the truth about things and men as the senses convey to us, yet this rule is merely the regularity of a dominant habit. It is possible for the mind, – and it would be natural for it, if it could be persuaded to liberate itself from its consent to the domination of matter, – to take direct cognisance of the objects of sense without the aid of the sense-organs. This is what happens in experiments of hypnosis and cognate psychological phenomena. Because our waking consciousness is determined and limited by the balance between mind and matter worked out by life in its evolution, this direct cognisance is usually impossible in our ordinary waking state and has therefore to be brought about by throwing the waking mind into a state of sleep which liberates the true or subliminal mind. Mind is then able to assert its true character as the one and all-sufficient sense and free to apply to the object of sense its pure and sovereign instead of its mixed and dependent action. Nor is this extension of faculty really impossible but only more difficult in our waking state, – as is known to all who have been able to go far enough in certain paths of psychological experiment.[21]

Sri Aurobindo

The mind of man and the Absolute

The mind much more intimately than the body and the life is the man, and the mind as it develops insists more and more on making the body and the life an instrument – an indispensable instrument and yet a considerable obstacle, otherwise there would be no problem – for its own characteristic satisfactions and self-realisation. The mind of man is not only a vital and physical, but an intellectual, aesthetic, ethical, psychic, emotional and dynamic intelligence, and in the sphere of each of its tendencies its highest and strongest nature is to strain towards some absolute of them which the frame of life will not allow it to capture wholly and embody and make here entirely real. The mental absolute of our aspiration remains as a partly grasped shining or fiery ideal which the mind can make inwardly very present to itself, inwardly imperative on its effort, and can even effectuate partly, but not compel all the facts of life into its image. *There is thus an absolute**, a high imperative of intellectual truth and reason sought for by our intellectual being; there is an absolute, an imperative of right and conduct aimed at by the ethical conscience; there is an absolute, an imperative of love, sympathy, compassion, oneness yearned after by our emotional and psychic nature; there is an absolute, an imperative of delight and beauty quivered to by the aesthetic soul; there is an absolute, an imperative of inner self-mastery and control of life laboured after by the dynamic will; all these are there together and impinge upon the absolute, the imperative of possession and pleasure and safe embodied existence insisted on by the vital and physical mind. And the human intelli-

* Emphasis ours. (Ed.)

gence, since it is not able to realise entirely any of these things, much less all of them together, erects in each sphere many standards and dharmas, standards of truth and reason, of right and conduct, of delight and beauty, of love, sympathy and oneness, of self-mastery and control, of self-preservation and possession and vital efficiency and pleasure, and tries to impose them on life. The absolute shining ideals stand far above and beyond our capacity and rare individuals approximate to them as best they can: the mass follow or profess to follow some less magnificent norm, some established possible and relative standard. Human life as a whole undergoes the attraction and yet rejects the ideal. Life resists in the strength of some obscure infinite of its own and wears down or breaks down any established mental and moral order. And this must be either because the two are quite different and disparate though meeting and interacting principles or because mind has not the clue to the whole reality of life. The clue must be sought in something greater, an unknown something above the mentality and morality of the human creature.[22]

Sri Aurobindo

Mind, Force and Consciousness

Where the Consciousness is divided in itself, as *in Mind*,* limiting itself in various centres, setting each to fulfil itself without knowledge of what is in other centres and of its relation to others, aware of things and forces in their apparent division and opposition to each other but not in their real unity, such will be the Force: it will be a life like that we are and see around us; it will be a clash and intertwining of indi-

* Emphasis ours. (Ed.)

Mind

vidual lives seeking each its own fulfilment without knowing its relation to others, a conflict and difficult accommodation of divided and opposing or differing forces and, in the mentality, a mixing, a shock and wrestle and insecure combination of divided and opposing or divergent ideas which cannot arrive at the knowledge of their necessity to each other or grasp their place as elements of that Unity behind which is expressing itself through them and in which their discords must cease. But where the Consciousness is in possession of both the diversity and the unity and the latter contains and governs the former, where it is aware at once of the Law, Truth and Right of the All and the Law, Truth and Right of the individual and the two become consciously harmonised in a mutual unity, where the whole nature of the consciousness is the One knowing itself as the Many and the Many knowing themselves as the One, there the Force also will be of the same nature: it will be a Life that consciously obeys the law of Unity and yet fulfils each thing in the diversity according to its proper rule and function; it will be a life in which all the individuals live at once in themselves and in each other as one conscious being in many souls, one power of Consciousness in many minds, one joy of Force working in many lives, one reality of Delight fulfilling itself in many hearts and bodies.[23]

Sri Aurobindo

The transformation of the human mentality

The visible imperfections and limitations of mind in the present stage of its evolution here we take as part of its very nature, but in fact the boundaries in which it is still penned are only temporary limits and measures of its still incomplete evolutionary advance; its defects of methods and means are faults of its immaturity and not proper to the constitution of its being; its achievement although extraordinary under the hampering conditions of the mental being weighed down by its instrumentation in an earthly body is far below and not beyond what will be possible to it in its illumined future. For mind is not in its very nature an inventor of errors, a father of lies bound down to a capacity of falsehood, wedded to its own mistakes and the leader of a stumbling life as it too largely is at present owing to our human shortcomings; it is in its origin a principle of light, an instrument put forth from the Supermind and, thought set to work within limits and even set to create limits, yet the limits are luminous borders for a special working, voluntary and purposive bounds, a service of the finite ever extending itself under the eye of infinity. It is this character of Mind that will reveal itself under the touch of Supermind and make human mentality an adjunct and a minor instrumentation of the supramental knowledge. It will even be possible for the mind no longer limited by the intellect to become capable of a sort of mental gnosis, a luminous reproduction of the truth in a diminished working extending the power of the Light not only to its own but to lower levels of consciousness in their climb towards self-transcendence. Overmind, Intuition, Illumined Mind and what I have called Higher Mind, these and other levels of a spiritualised and liberated mentality, will be able to reflect in the uplifted human mind and its purified and exalted feeling and force of life and action something of their powers and prepare the ascent of the soul to their own plateaus and peaks of an ascending existence. This is essentially the change which can be contemplated as a result of the new evolutionary order and it would mean a considerable extension of the evolutionary field itself and will answer the question as to the result on humanity of the advent of Supermind into the earth-nature.[24]

Sri Aurobindo

Mind in the process of divine knowledge

The mind will know nothing but the Brahman, think of nothing but the Brahman, the Life will move to embrace, enjoy nothing but the Brahman, the eye will see, the ear hear, the other senses sense nothing but the Brahman.

But is then a complete oblivion of the external the goal? Must the mind and senses recede inward and fall into an unending trance and the life be for ever stilled? This is possible, if the soul so wills, but it is not inevitable and indispensable. The Mind is cosmic, one in all the universe, so too are the Life, and the Sense, so too is Matter of the body; and when they exist in and for the Brahman only, they will not only know this but will sense, feel and live in that universal unity. Therefore to whatever thing they turn which to the individual sense and mind and life seems now external to them, there also it is not the mere form of things which they will know, think of, sense, embrace and enjoy, but always and only the Brahman. Moreover, the external will cease to exist for them, because nothing will be external but all things internal to us, even the whole world and all that is in it. For the limit of ego, the wall of individuality will break; the individual Mind will cease to know itself as individual, it will be conscious only of universal Mind one everywhere in which individuals are only knots of the one mentality; so the individual life will lose its sense of separateness and live only in and as the one life in which all individuals are simply whirls of the indivisible flood of Pranic activity, the very body and senses will be no longer conscious of a separated existence, but the real body which the man will feel himself to be physically will be the whole Earth and the whole universe and the whole indivisible form of things wheresoever existent, and the senses also will be converted to this principle of sensation so that even in what we call the external, the eye will see Brahman only in every sight, the ear will hear Brahman only in every sound, the inner and outer body will feel Brahman only in every touch and the touch itself as if internal in the greater body. The soul whose gods are thus converted to this supreme law and religion, will realise in the cosmos itself and in all its multiplicity the truth of the One besides whom there is no other or second. Moreover, becoming one with the formless and infinite, it will exceed the universe itself and see all the worlds not as external, not even as commensurate with itself, but as if within it.[25]

Sri Aurobindo

Mind in the higher realisation

And in fact, in the higher realisation it will not be Mind, Life, Sense of which even the mind, life and sense themselves will be originally aware, but rather that which constitutes them. By this process of constant visiting and divine touch and influence the Mind of the mind, that is to say, the superconscient Knowledge will take possession of the mental understanding and begin to turn all its vision and thinking into luminous stuff and vibration of light of the Supermind. So too the sense will be changed by the visitings of the Sense behind the sense and the whole sense-view of the universe itself will be altered so that the vital, mental and supramental will become visible to the senses with the physical only as their last, outermost and smallest result. So too the Life will become a superlife, a conscious movement of the infinite Conscious-Force; it will be impersonal, unlimited by any particular acts and enjoyment, unbound to their results, untroubled by the dualities or the touch of sin and suffering, grandiose, boundless, immortal. The material world itself will become for these gods a figure of the infinite, luminous and blissful Superconscient.[26]

Sri Aurobindo

Evolution [2]

I passed into a lucent still abode
    And saw as in a mirror crystalline
    An ancient Force ascending serpentine
The unhasting spirals of the aeonic road.
Earth was a cradle for the arriving god
    And man but a half-dark half-luminous sign
    Of the transition of the veiled Divine
From Matter's sleep and the tormented load
Of ignorant life and death to the Spirit's light.
    Mind liberated swam Light's ocean vast.
      And life escaped from its grey tortured line;
I saw Matter illumining its parent Night.
    The soul could feel into infinity cast
      Timeless God-bliss the heart incarnadine.[27]

                                  Sri Aurobindo

Mind is not the last possibility of consciousness.

Mind also has to call in a new principle beyond itself, freer than itself and more powerful.

In other words, Mind does not exhaust the possibilities of consciousness and therefore cannot be its last and highest expression. Mind tries to arrive at Truth and succeeds only in touching it imperfectly with a veil between; there must be in the nature of things a faculty or principle which sees the Truth unveiled, an eternal faculty of knowledge which corresponds to the eternal fact of the Truth. There is, says the Veda, such a principle; it is the Truth-Consciousness which sees the Truth directly and is in possession of it spontaneously. Mind labours to effect the will in it and succeeds only in accomplishing partially, with difficulty and insecurely the potentiality at which it works; there must be a faculty or principle of conscious effective force which corresponds to the unconscious automatic principle of self-fulfilment in Nature, and this principle must be sought for in the form of consciousness that exceeds Mind. Mind, finally aspires to seize and enjoy the essential delight-giving quality, the *rasa* of things, but it succeeds only in attaining to it indirectly, holding it in an imperfect grasp and enjoying it externally and fragmentarily; there must be a principle which can attain directly, hold rightly, enjoy intimately and securely. There is, says the Veda an eternal Bliss-consciousness which corresponds to the eternal *rasa* or essential delight-giving quality of all experience and is not limited by the insecure approximation of the sense in Mind.[28]

Sri Aurobindo

Mind is not sufficient to explain existence

Mind is not sufficient to explain existence in the universe. Infinite Consciousness must first translate itself into infinite faculty of Knowledge or, as we call it from our point of view, omniscience. But Mind is not a faculty of knowledge nor an instrument of omniscience; it is a faculty for the seeking of knowledge, for expressing as much as it can gain of it in certain forms of a relative thought and for using it towards certain capacities of action. Even when it finds, it does not possess; it only keeps a certain fund of current coin of Truth – not Truth itself – in the bank of Memory to draw upon according to its needs. For Mind is that which does not know, which tries to know and which never knows except as in a glass darkly. It is the power which interprets truth of universal existence for the practical uses of a certain order of things; it is not the power which knows and guides that existence and therefore it cannot be the power which created or manifested it....

Mind, as we know it, is a reflective mirror which receives presentations or images of a pre-existent Truth or Fact, either external to or at least vaster than itself. It represents to itself from moment to moment the phenomenon that is or has been. It possesses also the faculty of constructing in itself possible images other than those of the actual fact presented to it; that is to say, it represents to itself not only phenomenon that has been but also phenomenon that may be: it cannot, be it noted, represent to itself phenomenon that assuredly will be, except when it is an assured repetition of what is or has been. It has, finally, the faculty of forecasting new modifications which it seeks to construct out of the meeting of what has been and what may be, out of the fulfilled possibility and the unfulfilled, something that it sometimes succeeds in constructing more or less exactly, sometimes fails to realise, but usually finds cast into other forms than it forecasted and turned to other ends than it desired or intended.[29]

Sri Aurobindo

The mind and the inner being

Certainly, the mind and the inner being are consciousness. For human beings who have not got deeper into themselves, mind and consciousness are synonymous. Only when one becomes more aware of oneself by a growing consciousness, then one can see different degrees, kinds, powers of consciousness, mental, vital, physical, psychic, spiritual. The Divine has been described as Being, Consciousness, Ananda, even as a Consciousness (Chaitanya), as putting out a force or energy, Shakti that creates world. The mind is a modified consciousness that puts forth a mental energy. But the Divine can stand back from his energy and observe it at its work, it can be the Witness Purusha watching the works of Prakriti. Even the mind can do that – a man can stand back in his mind-consciousness and watch the mental energy doing things, thinking, planning, etc.; all introspection is based upon the fact that one can so divide oneself into a consciousness that observes and an energy that acts. These are quite elementary things supposed to be known to everybody. Anybody can do that merely by a little practice; anybody who observes his own thoughts, feelings, actions, has begun doing it already. In yoga we make the division complete, that is all.[30]

Sri Aurobindo

THE MINDS OF MAN

The Mother

Man, the Thinking Animal

A trifling unit in a boundless plan
   Amidst the enormous insignificance
   Of the unpeopled cosmos' fire-whirl dance,
Earth, as by accident, engendered man:

A creature of his own grey ignorance,
   A mind half-shadow and half-gleam, a breath
   That wrestles, captive in a world of death,
To live some lame brief years, Yet his advance,

Attempt of a divinity within,
   A consciousness in the inconscient Night,
   To realise its own supernal Light
Confronts the ruthless forces of the Unseen.

Aspiring to godhead from insensible day
He travels slow-footed towards the eternal day.[31]

                                      Sri Aurobindo

Classification

*Mother, what does "vital mind" mean?**

Well, you see, naturally these words are used for classification in order to make oneself understood; but truly, each part of the being is itself divided into four. There is a physical mind, a physical vital and a physical physical, and there is even a physical psychic which is behind. Well, there is a vital mind, a vital vital, a vital physical and also a vital psychic which is behind, hidden. And there is a mental mind, a vital mind, and a physical mind and a psychic which is hidden behind. And each one corresponds to a particular kind of activity, and also to a particular region, a zone of consciousness and being. And these zones or inner dimensions correspond to outer zones and dimensions, universal, or terrestrial if you like, to simplify the problem. There is a mental mind within you, there is a mental mind in the terrestrial atmosphere; and – how shall I put it? – the density of these inner and outer regions is the same, the vibratory mode is identical.[32]

The Mother

The mixture of the minds

The average human being even now is in his inward existence as crude and undeveloped as was the bygone primitive man in his outward life. But as soon as we go deep within ourselves, – and Yoga means a plunge into all the multiple

---

* The Mother had been commenting Sri Aurobindo's *Bases on Yoga* (Ed.)

profundities of the soul, – we find ourselves subjectively, as man in his growth has found himself objectively, surrounded by a whole complex world which we have to know and to conquer.

The most disconcerting discovery is to find that every part of us – intellect, will, sense-mind, nervous or desire self, the heart, the body – has each, as it were, its own complex individuality and natural formation independent of the rest; it neither agrees with itself nor with the others nor with the representative ego which is the shadow cast by some central and centralising self on our superficial ignorance. We find that we are composed not of one but many personalities and each has its own demands and differing nature. *Our being is a roughly constituted chaos into which we have to introduce the principle of a divine order.** Moreover, we find that inwardly too, no less than outwardly, we are not alone in the world; the sharp separateness of our ego was no more than a strong imposition and delusion; we do not exist in ourselves, we do not really live apart in an inner privacy or solitude. Our mind is a receiving, developing and modifying machine into which there is being constantly passed from moment to moment a ceaseless foreign flux, a streaming mass of disparate materials from above, from below, from outside. Much more than half our thoughts and feelings are not our own in the sense that they take form out of ourselves; of hardly anything can it be said that it is truly original to our nature. A large part comes to us from others or from the environment, whether as raw material or as manufactured imports; but still more largely they come from universal Nature here or from other worlds and planes and their beings and powers and in-

---

* Emphasis ours. (Ed.)

fluences; for we are overtopped and environed by other planes of consciousness, mind planes, life planes, subtle matter planes, from which our life and action here are fed, or fed on, pressed, dominated, made use of for the manifestation of their forms and forces. The difficulty of our separate salvation is immensely increased by this complexity and manifold openness and subjection to the in-streaming energies of the universe. Of all this we have to take account, to deal with it, to know what is the secret stuff of our nature and its constituent and resultant motions and to create in it all a divine centre and a true harmony and luminous order.[33]

Sri Aurobindo

THE PHYSICAL MIND

The Physical Mind

The physical mind is that part of the mind which is concerned with the physical things only – it depends on the sense-mind, sees only objects, external actions, draws its ideas from the data given by external things, infers from them only and knows no other Truth until it is enlightened from above.[34]

Sri Aurobindo

At the outset man lives in his physical mind

At the outset man lives in his physical mind which perceives the actual, the physical, the objective and accepts it as fact and this fact as self-evident truth beyond question; whatever is not actual, not physical, not objective it regards as unreal or unrealised, only to be accepted as entirely real when it has succeeded in becoming actual, becoming a physical fact, becoming objective: its own being too it regards as an objective fact, warranted to be real by its existence in a visible and sensible body; all other subjective beings and things it accepts on the same evidence in so far as they can become objects of our external consciousness or acceptable to that part of the reason which builds upon the data supplied by that consciousness and relies upon them as the one solid basis of knowledge. Physical Science is a vast extension of this mentality: it corrects the errors of the sense and pushes beyond the first limitations of the sense-mind by discovering means of bringing facts and objects not seizable by our corporeal organs into the field of objectivity, but it has the same standard of reality, the objective; the physical actuality; its test of the real is possibility of verification by positive reason and objective evidence.[35]

Sri Aurobindo

The stand of the physical mind

Our physical mind is not the whole of us nor, even though it dominates almost the whole of our surface consciousness, the best or greatest part of us; reality cannot be restricted to a sole field of this narrowness or to the dimensions known within its rigid circle.[36]

*

For the physical mind takes its stand on matter and the material world, on the body and the bodily life, on sense-experience and on a normal practical mentality and its experience. All that is not of this order, the physical mind builds up as a restricted superstructure dependent upon the external sense-mentality. Even so, it regards these higher contents of life as either helpful adjuncts or a superfluous but pleasant luxury of imaginations, feelings and thought-abstractions, not as inner realities; or, even if it receives them as realities, it does not feel them concretely and substantially in their own proper substance, subtler than the physical substance and its grosser concreteness, – it treats them as a subjective, less substantial extension from physical realities.[37]

Sri Aurobindo

*

In the West the physical mind is too dominant, so that

the psychic does not so easily get a chance – except of course in exceptional people.[38]

Sri Aurobindo

Response of the physical mind

The terms Manas, etc. belongs to the ordinary psychology applied to the surface consciousness. In our yoga we adopt a different classification – based on the yogic experience. What answers to this movement of the Manas there would be two separate things – a part of the physical mind communicating with the physical-vital. It receives from the physical senses and transmits to the Buddhi – i.e., to some part or other of the Thought-Mind. It receives back from the Buddhi and transmits idea and will to the organs of sensation and action. All that is indispensable in the ordinary action of the consciousness. But in the ordinary consciousness everything gets mixed up together and there is no clear order or rule. In the yoga one becomes aware of the different parts and their proper action, and puts each in its place and to its proper action under the control of the higher Consciousness or else under the control of the Divine Power. Afterwards all gets surcharged with the spiritual consciousness and there is an automatic right perception and right action of the different parts because they are controlled entirely from above and do not falsify or resist or confuse its dictates.[39]

Sri Aurobindo

The limitations of the physical mind

There are different orders of reality; the objective and physical is only one order. It is convincing to the physical or externalising mind because it is directly obvious to the senses, while of the subjective and the supraphysical that mind has no means of knowledge except from fragmentary signs and data and inferences which are at every step liable to error. Our subjective movements and inner experiences are a domain of happenings as real as any outward physical happenings; but if the individual mind can know something of its own phenomena by direct experience, it is ignorant of what happens in the consciousness of others except by analogy with its own or such signs, data, inferences as its outward observation can give it. I am therefore inwardly real to myself, but the invisible life of others has only an indirect reality to me except in so far as it impinges on my own mind, life and senses. This is the limitation of the physical mind of man, and it creates in him a habit of believing entirely only in the physical and of doubting or challenging all that does not come into accord with his own experience or his own scope of understanding or square with his own standard or sum of established knowledge.[40]

Sri Aurobindo

The physical mind and work

Think of your work only when it is being done, not before and not after.

Do not let your mind go back on a work that is finished. It belongs to the past and all re-handling of it is a waste of power.

Do not let your mind labour in anticipation on a work that has to be done. The Power that acts in you will see to it at its own time.

These two habits of the mind belong to a past function-

The Physical Mind

ing that the transforming Force is presssing to remove and the physical mind's persistence in them is the cause of your strain and fatigue. If you can remember to let your mind work only when its action is needed, the strain will lessen and disappear. This is indeed the transitional movement before the supramental working takes possession of the physical mind and brings into it the spontaneous action of the Light.[41]

Sri Aurobindo

The action of the physical mind

In physical mind there can be an action of intelligent reasoning and coordination which is a delegation from the Buddhi and would perhaps not be attributed to the Manas by the old psychology. Still the larger part of the action of physical mind corresponds to that of Manas, but it comprises also much of what we would attribute to vital mind and to the nervous being. It is a little difficult to equate this old nomenclature with that of this yoga, for the former takes the mixed action of the surface and tries to analyse it – while in this yoga what is mixed together on the surface gets separated and seen in the light of the deeper working behind which is hidden from the surface awareness. So we have to adopt a different classification.[42]

Sri Aurobindo

The physical mind has first to open

The physical mind has first to open to the higher consciousness – its limitations are then removed and it admits what is supraphysical and begins to see things in harmony with the higher knowledge. It becomes an instrument for externalising that knowledge in the pragmatic perceptions and actions of the physical life. It sees things as they are and deals with them according to the larger Truth with an automatic rightness of perception and will and reaction to impacts.[43]

Sri Aurobindo

Change in the physical mind

It [the physical mind being intuitivised] is when instead of seeing things as they appear to the external mind and senses, one begins to see things about them with a subtler physical mind and sense – e.g. seeing intuitively what is to be done, how to do it, what the object (even so-called inanimate objects) wants or needs, what is likely to happen next (or sometimes sure to happen), what forces are at play on the physical plane etc. etc. Even the body becomes intuitively conscious in this way, feels without being told by the mind what it has to do, what it has to avoid, what is near it or coming to it (though unseen) etc. etc.[44]

*

Certainly. It [the changed physical mind] can press upon it [the physical vital] the true attitude and feeling, make the incoming of the wrong suggestions and impulsions more difficult and give full force to the true movements. This action of the physical mind is indispensable for the change of the whole physical consciousness even to the most material, though for that the enlightening of the subconscient is indispensable.[45]

Sri Aurobindo

The surface mind

In our surface mind we have no direct means of knowing even other men who are of our own kind and have a similar mentality and are vitally and physically built on the same model. We can acquire a general knowledge of the human mind and the human body and apply it to them with the aid of the many constant and habitual outer signs of the human inner movements with which we are familiar; these summary judgments can be further eked out by our experience of personal character and habits, by instinctive application of what self-knowledge we have to our understanding and judgment of others, by inference from speech and conduct, by insight of observation and insight of sympathy. But the results are always incomplete and very frequently deceptive: our inferences are as often as not erroneous constructions, our interpretation of the outward signs a mistaken guess-work, our application of general knowledge or our self-knowledge baffled by elusive factors of personal difference, our very insight uncertain and unrealiable. Human beings therefore live as strangers to each other, at best tied by a very partial sympathy and mutual experience; we do not know enough, do not know as well as we know ourselves, – and that itself is little, – even those nearest to us.[46]

Sri Aurobindo

*

We exist superficially by a becoming in Time; but here again out of that becoming in Time the surface mind, which we call ourselves, is ignorant of all the long past and the long future, aware only of the little life which it remembers and not of all even of that; for much of it is lost to its observation, much to its memory.[47]

Sri Aurobindo

The place of the sense-mind

Mind, life and body are the three powers of our lower nature. But they cannot be taken quite separately because the life acts as a link and gives its character to body and to a great extent to our mentality. Our body is a living body; the life-force mingles in and determines all its functionings. Our mind too is largely a mind of life, a mind of physical sensation; only in its higher functions is it normally capable of something more than the workings of a physical mentality subjected to life.... This mentality is pervaded by the life-force, which becomes here an instrument for psychic consciousness of life and psychic action on life. Every fibre of the sense mind and basic consciousness is shot through with the action of this psychic prana, it is a nervous or vital and physical mentality. Even the buddhi and ego are over-powered by it, although they have the capacity of raising the mind beyond subjection to this vital, nervous and physical psychology. This combination creates in us the sensational desire-soul which is the chief obstacle to a higher human as well as to the still greater divine perfection. Finally, above our present conscious mentality is a secret supermind which is the proper means and native seat of that perfection.[48]

Sri Aurobindo

The sense-mind (Manas)

In a sense all our experience is psychological since even what we receive by the senses has no meaning or value to us till it is translated into the terms of the sense-mind, the Manas of Indian philosophical terminology. Manas, say our philosophers, is the sixth sense. But we may even say that it is the only sense and that the others, vision, hearing, touch, smell, taste are merely specialisations of the sense-mind which, although it normally uses the sense-organs for the basis of its experience, yet exceeds them and is capable of a direct experience proper to its own inherent action. As a result psychological experience, like the cognitions of the reason, is capable in man of a double action, mixed or dependent, pure or sovereign. Its mixed action takes place usually when the mind seeks to become aware of the external world, the object; the pure action when it seeks to become aware of itself, the subject. In the former activity, it is dependent on the senses and forms its perceptions in accordance with their evidence; in the latter it acts in itself and is aware of things directly by a sort of identity with them. We are thus aware of our emotions; we are aware of anger, as has been acutely said, because we become anger. We are thus aware also of our own existence; and here the nature of experience as knowledge by identity becomes apparent. In reality, all experience is in its secret nature knowledge by identity; but its true character is hidden from us because we have separated ourselves from the rest of the world by exclusion, by the distinction of ourself as subject and everything else as object, and we are compelled to develop processes and organs by which we may again enter into communion with all that we have excluded. We have to replace direct knowledge through conscious identity by an indirect knowledge which appears to be caused by physical contact and mental sympathy. This limitation is a fundamental creation of the ego and an instance of the manner in which it has proceeded throughout, starting from an original falsehood and covering over the true truth of things by contingent falsehoods which become for us practical truths of relation.[49]

Sri Aurobindo

The sense-mind and the powers of mind

Manas, sense-mind, is the essentiality, emerging from the basic consciousness, which makes up the whole of what we call sense. Sight, hearing, taste, smell, touch are really properties of the mind, not of the body; but the physical mind which we ordinarily use, limits itself to a translation into sense of so much of the outer impacts as it receives through the nervous system and the physical organs. But the inner Manas has also a subtle sight, hearing, power of contact of its own which is not dependent on the physical organs. And it has, moreover, a power not only of direct communication of mind with object – leading even at a high pitch of action to a sense of the contents of an object within or beyond the physical range, – but direct communication also of mind with mind. Mind is able too to alter, modify, inhibit the incidence, values, intensities of sense impacts. These powers of the mind we do not ordinarily use or develop; they remain subliminal and emerge sometimes in an irregular and fitful action, more readily in some minds than in others, or come to the surface in abnormal states of the being. They are the basis of clairvoyance, clairaudience, transference of thought and impulse, telepathy, most of the more ordinary kinds of occult powers,

The Physical Mind

– so called, though these are better described less mystically as powers of the now subliminal action of the Manas. The phenomena of hypnotism and many others depend upon the action of this subliminal sense-mind; not that it alone constitutes all the elements of the phenomena, but it is the first supporting means of intercourse, communication and response, though much of the actual operation belongs to an inner Buddhi. Mind physical, mind supraphysical, – we have and can use this double sense mentality.[50]

Sri Aurobindo

Purification of the function of the sense-mind

Equally must the sense-mind be stilled and taught to leave the function of thought to the mind that judges and understands. When the understanding in us stands back from the action of the sense-mind and repels its intermiscence, the latter detaches itself from the understanding and can be watched in its separate action. It then reveals itself as a constantly swirling and eddying undercurrent of habitual concepts, associations, perceptions, desires without any real sequence, order or principle of light. It is a constant repetition in a circle unintelligent and unfruitful. Ordinarily the human understanding accepts this undercurrent and tries to reduce it to a partial order and sequence; but by so doing it becomes itself subject to it and partakes of that disorder, restlessness, unintelligent subjection to habit and blind purposeless repetition which makes the ordinary human reason a misleading, limited and even frivolous and futile instrument. There is nothing to be done with this fickle, restless, violent and disturbing factor but to get rid of it whether by detaching it and then reducing it to stillness or by giving a concentration and singleness to the thought by which it will of itself reject this alien and confusing element.[51]

Sri Aurobindo

The proper function of the sense-mind

The proper function of the life-energy is to do what it is bidden by the divine principle in us, to reach to and enjoy what is given to it by that indwelling Divine and not to desire at all. The proper function of the sense-mind is to lie open passively, luminously to the contacts of Life and transmit their sensations and the *rasa* or right taste and principle of delight in them to the higher function; but interfered with by the attractions and repulsions, the acceptances and refusals, the satisfactions and dissatisfactions, the capacities and incapacities of the life-energy in the body it is, to begin with, limited in its scope and, secondly, forced in these limits to associate itself with all these discords of the life in Matter. It becomes an instrument for pleasure and pain instead of for delight of existence.[52]

Sri Aurobindo

THE VITAL MIND

The Vital mind as part of the nature

There is a part of the nature which I have called the vital mind; the function of this mind is not to think and reason, to perceive, consider and find out or value things, for that is the function of the thinking mind proper, *buddhi*, – but to plan or dream or imagine what can be done. It makes formations for the future which the will can try to carry out if opportunity and circumstances become favourable or even it can work to make them favourable. In men of action this faculty is prominent and a leader of their nature; great men of action always have it in a very high measure. But even if one is not a man of action or practical realisation or if circumstances are not favourable or one can do only small and ordinary things, this vital mind is there. It acts in them on a small scale, or if it needs some sense of largeness, what it does very often is to plan in the void, knowing that it cannot realise its plans or else to imagine big things, stories, adventures, great doings in which oneself is the hero or the creator.[53]

*

[The vital mind] is a mind of dynamic (not rationalising) will, action, desire – occupied with force and achievement and satisfaction and possession, enjoyment and suffering, giving and taking, growth, expansion, success and failure, good fortune and ill fortune etc., etc.[54]

*

That is the ordinary activity of the vital mind which is always imagining and thinking and planing what to do about this and how to arrange about that. It has obviously its utility in human nature and human action, but acts in a random and excessive way without discipline, economy of its powers or concentration on the things that have really to be done.[55]

Sri Aurobindo

Life

Mystic Miracle, daughter of Delight,
   Life, thou ecstasy,
Let the radius of thy flight
   Be eternity.

On thy wings thou bearest high
   Glory and disdain,
Godhead and mortality,
   Ecstasy and pain.

Take me in thy wild embrace
   Without weak reserve
Body dire and unveiled face;
   Faint not, Life, nor swerve.

All thy bliss I would explore,
   All thy tyranny.
Cruel like the lion's roar,
   Sweet like springtide be.

Like a Titan I would take,
   Like a God enjoy,
Like a man contend and make,
   Revel like a boy.

More I will not ask of thee,
   Nor my fate would choose;
King or conquered let me be,
   Live or lose.

Even in rags I am a god;
   Fallen, I am divine;
High I triumph when down-trod,
   Long I live when slain.[56]

Sri Aurobindo

Four parts of the vital being

There are four parts of the vital being – first, the mental vital which gives a mental expression by thought, speech or otherwise to the emotions, desires, passions, sensations and other movements of the vital being; the emotional vital which is the seat of various feelings, such as love, joy, sorrow, hatred, and the rest; the central vital which is the seat of the stronger vital longings and reactions, e.g. ambition, pride, fear, love of fame, attractions and repulsions, desires and passions of various kinds and the field of many vital energies; last, the lower vital which is occupied with small desires and feelings, such as make the greater part of daily life, e.g. food desire, sexual desire, small likings, dislikings, vanity, quarrels, love of praise, anger at blame, little wishes of all kinds – and a numberless host of other things. Their respective seats are: (1) the region from the throat to the heart, (2) the heart (it is a double centre, belonging in front to the emotional and vital and behind to the psychic), (3) from the heart to the navel, (4) below the navel.[57]

Sri Aurobindo

The true vital being

When the true vital being comes forward, it is something wide and strong and calm, an unmoved and powerful warrior for the Divine and the Truth, repelling all enemies, bringing in a true strength and force, and opening the vital to the greater consciousness above.[58]

Sri Aurobindo

The Vital mind as part of the vital being

The vital mind is that part of the vital being which builds, plans, imagines, arranges things and thoughts according to the life-pushes, desires, will to power or possession, will to action, emotions, vital ego reactions of the nature. It must be distinguished from the reasoning will which plans and arranges things according to the dictates of the thinking mind proper, the discriminating reason or according to the mental intuition or a direct insight and judgment. The vital mind uses thought for the service not of reason but of life-push and life-power and when it calls in reasoning it uses that for justifying the dictates of these powers, imposes their dictates on the reason instead of governing by a discriminating will the action of the life-forces. This higher vital with all its parts is situated in the chest and has the cardiac centre as its main stronghold governing all this part down to the navel. I need not say anything about the emotional nature, for its character and movements are known to all. From the navel downwards is the reign of the vital passions and sensations and all the small life-impulses that constitute the bulk of the ordinary human life and character. This is what we call the lower vital nature. The Muladhara is the main support of the physical consciousness and the material parts of the nature.[59]

Sri Aurobindo

The Vital mind proper

Vital mind proper is a sort of mediator between vital emotion, desire, impulsion, etc. and the mental proper. It expresses the desires, feelings, emotions, passions, ambitions, possessive and active tendencies of the vital and throws them

The Vital Mind

into mental forms (the pure imaginations or dreams of greatness, happiness, etc. in which men indulge are one peculiar form of the vital-mind activity). There is still a lower stage of the mental in the vital which merely expresses the vital stuff without subjecting it to any play of intelligence. It is through this mental vital that the vital passions, impulses, desires rise up and get into the Buddhi and either cloud or distort it.

As the vital Mind is limited by the vital view and feeling of things (while the dynamic Intelligence is not, for it acts by the idea and reason), so the mind in the physical or mental physical is limited by the physical view and experience of things, it mentalises the experiences brought by the contacts of outward life and things, and does not go beyond that (though it can do that much very cleverly), unlike the externalising mind which deals with them more from the reason and its higher intelligence. But in practice these two *usually get mixed together**. The mechanical mind is a much lower action of the mental physical which, left to itself, would only repeat customary ideas and record the natural reflexes of the physical consciousness to the contacts of outward life and things.

The *lower** vital as distinguished from the *higher* is concerned only with the small greeds, small desires, small passions, etc. which make up the daily stuff of life for the ordinary sensational man – while the vital-physical proper is the nervous being giving vital reflexes to contacts of things with the physical consciousness.[60]

Sri Aurobindo

---

* Emphasis ours. (Ed.)

The emotional mind

Similarly the emotional mind compelled to take note of all these *discords** and subject itself to their emotional reactions becomes a hurtling field of joy and grief, love and hatred, wrath, fear, struggle, aspiration, disgust, likes, dislikes, indifferences, content, discontent, hopes, disappointments, gratitude, revenge and all the stupendous play of passion which is the drama of life in the world. This chaos we call our soul. But the real soul, the real psychic entity which for the most part we see little of and only a small minority in mankind has developed, is an instrument of pure love, joy and the luminous reaching out to fusion and unity with God and our fellow-creatures. This psychic entity is covered up by the play of the mentalised Prana or desire-mind which we mistake for the soul; the emotional mind is unable to mirror the real soul in us, the Divine in our hearts, and is obliged instead to mirror the desire-mind.[61]

Sri Aurobindo

Purification of the vital mind

These intermediary parts are the emotional mind, the receptive sensational mind and the active sensational mind or mind of dynamic impulse. They all hang together in a strongly knotted interaction. The deformation of the emotional mind hinges upon the duality of liking and disliking, *rāga-dveśa*, emotional attraction and repulsion. All the complexity of our

---

* "*discords*": Sri Aurobindo means discords between the sense-mind (as part of the physical mind), the emotional mind (as part of the vital mind) and the thought mind (as part of the mental mind). Emphasis ours. (Ed.)

The Vital Mind

emotions and their tyranny over the soul arise from the habitual responses of the soul of desire in the emotions and sensations to these attractions and repulsions. Love and hatred, hope and fear, grief and joy all have their founts in this one source. We like, love, welcome, hope for, joy in whatever our nature, the first habit of our being, or else a formed (often perverse) habit, the second nature of our being, presents to the mind as pleasant, *priyam*; we hate, dislike, fear, have repulsion from or grief of whatever it presents to us as unpleasant *apriyam*. This habit of the emotional nature gets into the way of the intelligent will and makes it often a helpless slave of the emotional being or at least prevents it from exercising a free judgment and government of the nature. This deformation has to be corrected. By getting rid of desire in the psychic prana and its intermiscence in the emotional mind, we facilitate the correction. For then attachment, which is the strong bond of the heart, falls away from the heart-strings; the involuntary habit of *rāga-dveśa*, but, not being made obstinate by attachment, it can be dealth with more easily by the will and the intelligence. The restless heart can be conquered and get rid of the habit of attraction and repulsion.[62]

Sri Aurobindo

*

What is needed is a general plasticity of the mind, the vital, the physical consciousness, a readiness to give up all attachment to these things, to accept whatever the higher consciousness brings down with it however contrary to one's own received ideas, feelings, habits of nature. The greater the plasticity in any part of the nature, the less the resistance there.[63]

Sri Aurobindo

For man's mind is the dupe of his animal self

For man's mind is the dupe of his animal self;
   Hoping its lusts to win,
He harbours within him a grisly Elf
   Enamoured of sorrow and sin.

The grey Elf shudders from heaven's flame
   And from all things glad and pure;
Only by pleasure and passion and pain
   His drama can endure.[64]

                              Sri Aurobindo

Vital mind as an instrument of desire

But man also has a life-mind, a vital mentality which is an instrument of desire: this is not satisfied with the actual, it is a dealer in possibilities; it has the passion for novelty and is seeking always to extend the limits of experience for the satisfaction of desire, for enjoyment, for an enlarged self-affirmation and aggrandisement of its terrain of power and profit. It desires, enjoys, possesses actualities, but it hunts also after unrealised possibilities, is ardent to materialise them, to possess and enjoy them also. It is not satisfied with the physical and objective only, but seeks too a subjective, an imaginative, a purely emotive satisfaction and pleasure. If there were not this factor, the physical mind of man left to itself would live like the animal, accepting his first actual physical life and its limits as his whole possibility, moving in material Nature's established order and asking for nothing beyond it. But this *vital mind,* this unquiet *life-will** comes in with its demands and disturbs this inertia or routine satisfaction which lives penned within the bounds of actuality; it enlarges always desire and craving, creates a dissatisfaction, an unrest, a seeking for something more than what life seems able to give it: it brings about a vast enlargement of the field of physical actuality by the actualisation of our unrealised possibilities, but also a constant demand for more and always more, a quest for new worlds to conquer, an incessant drive towards an exceeding of the bounds of circumstance and a self-exceeding.[65]

Sri Aurobindo

---

* Emphasis ours (Ed.)

The rejection of the desire-mind

The desire-mind must also be rejected from the instrument of thought and this is best done by the detachment of the Purusha from thought and opinion itself. Of this we have already had occasion to speak when we considered in what consists the integral purification of the being. For all this movement of knowledge which we are describing is a method of purification and liberation whereby entire and final self-knowledge becomes possible, a progressive self-knowledge being itself the instrument of the purification and liberation. The method with the thought-mind will be the same as with all the rest of the being. The Purusha, having used the thought-mind for release from identification with the life and body and with the mind of desire and sensations and emotions, will turn round upon the thought-mind itself and will say "This too I am not; I am not the thought or the thinker; all these ideas, opinions, speculations, strivings of the intellect, its predilections, preferences, dogmas, doubts, self-corrections are not myself; all this is only a working of Prakriti which takes place in the thought-mind." Thus a division is created between the mind that thinks and wills and the mind that observes and the Purusha becomes the witness only; he sees, he understands the process and laws of his thought, but detaches himself from it. Then as the master of the sanction he withdraws his past sanction from the tangle of the mental undercurrent and the reasoning intellect and causes both to cease from their importunities. He becomes liberated from subjection to the thinking mind and capable of the utter silence.

For perfection there is necessary also the resumption by the Purusha of his position as the lord of his Nature and the will to replace the mere mental undercurrent and intellect by the truth-conscious thought that lightens from above. But the silence is necessary; in the silence and not in the thought we shall find the Self, we shall become aware of it, not merely conceive it, and we shall withdraw out of the mental Purusha into that which is the source of the mind. But for this withdrawal a final liberation is needed, the release from the ego-sense in the mind.[66]

Sri Aurobindo

Vital mind, duality and the psychic being

The duality begins with conscious life and emerges fully with the development of mind in life; the vital mind, the mind of desire and sensation, is the creator of the sense of evil and of the fact of evil.... The sensational values of good and evil are inherent in the form of pain and pleasure, vital satisfaction and vital frustration, but the mental idea, the moral response of the mind to these values are a creation of the human being. It does not follow, as might be hastily inferred, that they are unrealities, mental constructions only, and that the only true way to receive the activities of Nature is either a neutral indifference or an equal acceptance or, intellectually, an admission of all that she may do as a divine or a natural law in which everything is impartially admissible. That is indeed one side of the truth: there is an infrarational truth of Life and Matter which is impartial and neutral and admits all things as facts of Nature and serviceable for the creation, preservation or destruction of life, three necessary movements of the universal Energy which are all connectedly indispensable and, each in its own place, of equal value. There is too a truth of the detached reason which can look on all that is thus admitted by Nature as serviceable to her processes in life and matter and observe everything that is with an unmoved neutral impartiality and acceptance; this is a philosophic and scientific reason that witnesses and seeks to understand but considers it futile to judge the activities of the cosmic Energy. There is too a suprarational truth formulating itself in spiritual experience which can observe the play of universal possibility, accept all impartially as the true and natural features and consequences of a world of ignorance and inconscience or admit all with calm and compassion as a part of the divine working, but, while it awaits the awakening of a higher consciousness and knowledge as the sole escape from what presents itself as evil, is ready with help and intervention where that is truly helpful and possible.

... What then is this spiritual or psychic witness or what is to it the value of the sense of good and evil? It may be maintained that the one use of the sense of sin and evil is that the embodied being may become aware of the nature of this world of inconscience and ignorance, awake to a knowledge of its evil and suffering and the relative nature of its good and happiness and turn away from it to that which is absolute.

... For much more than the mind or life which can turn either to good or to evil, it is the soul-personality, the psychic being, which insists on the distinction, though in a larger sense than the mere moral difference. It is the soul in us which turns always towards Truth, Good and Beauty, because it is by these things that it itself grows in stature; the rest, their opposites, are a necessary part of experience, but have to be outgrown in the spiritual increase of the being. The fundamental psychic entity in us has the delight of life and all experience as part of the progressive manifestation of the spirit,

The Vital Mind

but the very principle of its delight of life is to gather out of all contacts and happenings their secret divine sense and essence, a divine use and purpose so that by experience our mind and life may grow out of the Inconscience towards a supreme consciousness, out of the divisions of the Ignorance towards an integralising consciousness and knowledge. It is there for that and it pursues from life to life its ever-increasing upward tendency and insistence; the growth of the soul is a growth out of darkness into light, out of falsehood into truth, out of suffering into its own supreme and universal Ananda. The soul's perception of good and evil may not coincide with the mind's artificial standards, but it has a deeper sense, a sure discrimination of what points to the higher Light and what points away from it. It is true that as the inferior light is below good and evil, so the superior spiritual light is beyond good and evil; but this is not in the sense of admitting all things with an impartial neutrality or of obeying equally the impulses of good and evil, but in the sense that a higher law of being intervenes in which there is no longer any place or utility for these values. There is a self-law of supreme Truth which is above all standards; there is a supreme and universal Good inherent, intrinsic, self-existent, self-aware, self-moved and determined, infinitely plastic with the pure plasticity of the luminous consciousness of the supreme Infinite.[67]

Sri Aurobindo

Inner experience: the aesthetic mind

Our whole being ought to demand God and not only our illumined eye of knowledge. For since each principle in us is only a manifestation of the Self, each can get back to its reality and have the experience of it. We can have a mental experience of the Self and seize as concrete realities all those apparently abstract things that to the mind constitute existence – consciousness, force, delight and their manifold forms and workings: thus the mind is satisfied of God. We can have an emotional experience of the Self through Love and through emotional delight, love and delight of the Self in us, of the Self in the universal and of the Self in all with whom we have relations: thus the heart is satisfied of God. We can have an aesthetic experience of the Self in beauty, a delight-perception and taste of the absolute reality all-beautiful in everything whether created by ourselves or Nature in its appeal to the aesthetic mind and the senses; thus the sense is satisfied of God. We can have even the vital, nervous experience and practically the physical sense of the Self in all life and formation and in all workings of powers, forces, energies that operate through us or others or in the world: thus the life and the body are satisfied of God.[68]

Sri Aurobindo

The vital mind and evolution

This life-mentality is supported by our secret subliminal vital being and is in veiled contact with a life world to which it can easily open and so feel the unseen dynamic forces and realities behind the material universe. ... The vital man, moulded consciously or unconsciously by these influences, is the man of desire and sensation, the man of force and action, the man of passion and emotion, the kinetic individual: he may and does lay great stress on the material existence, but he gives it, even when most preoccupied with its present actualities, a push for life-experience, for force of realisation, for life-extension, for life-power, for life-affirmation and life-expansion which is Nature's first impetus towards enlargement of the being; at a highest intensity of this life-impetus, he becomes the breaker of bonds, the seeker of new horizons, the disturber of the past and present in the interest of future. He has a mental life which is often enslaved to the vital force and its desires and passions, and it is these he seeks to satisfy through the mind; but when he interests himself strongly in mental things, he can become the mental adventurer, the opener of the way to new mind-formations or the fighter for an idea, the sensitive type of artist, the dynamic poet of life or the prophet or champion of a cause. The vital mind is kinetic and therefore a great force in the working of evolutionary Nature.[69]

Sri Aurobindo

Release from the desire-mind and the emotional mind

The mental Purusha has to separate himself from association and self-identification with this desire-mind. He has to say "I am not this thing that struggles and suffers, grieves and rejoices, loves and hates, hopes and is baffled, is angry and afraid and cheerful and depressed, a thing of vital moods and emotional passions. All these are merely workings and habits of Prakriti in the sensational and emotional mind." The mind then draws back from its emotions and becomes with these, as with the bodily movements and experiences, the observer or witness. There is again an inner cleavage. There is this emotional mind in which these moods and passions continue to occur according to the habit of the modes of Nature and there is the observing mind which sees them, studies and understands but is detached from them. It observes them as if in a sort of action and play on a mental stage of personages other than itself, at first with interest and a habit of relapse into identification, then with entire calm and detachment, and, finally, attaining not only to calm but to the pure delight of its own silent existence, with a smile at their unreality as at the imaginary joys and sorrows of a child who is playing and loses himself in the play. Secondly, it becomes aware of itself as master of the sanction who by his withdrawal of sanction can make this play to cease. When the sanction is withdrawn, another significant phenomenon takes place; the emotional mind becomes normally calm and pure and free from these reactions, and even when they come, they no longer rise from within but seem to fall on it as impressions from outside to which its fibres are still able to respond; but this habit of response dies away and the emotional mind is in time entirely liberated from the passions which it has renounced. Hope and fear, joy and grief, liking and disliking, attraction and repulsion, content and discontent, gladness and depression, horror and wrath and fear and disgust and shame and the passions of love and hatred fall away from the liberated psychic being.[70]

Sri Aurobindo

The vital mind can be a great force

[Man] has a mental life which is often enslaved to the vital force and its desires and passions, and it is these he seeks to satisfy through the mind: but when he interests himself strongly in mental things, he can become the mental adventurer, the opener of the way to new mind-formations or the fighter for an idea, the sensitive type of artist, the dynamic poet of life or the prophet or champion of a cause. The vital mind is kinetic and therefore a great force in the working of evolutionary Nature.[71]

Sri Aurobindo

Bride of the Fire

Bride of the Fire, clasp me now close, –
  Bride of the Fire!
I have shed the bloom of the earthly rose,
  I have slain desire.

Beauty of the Light, surround my life, –
  Beauty of the Light!
I have sacrificed longing and parted from grief,
  I can bear thy delight.

Image of ecstasy, thrill and enlace, –
  Image of bliss!
I would see only thy marvellous face,
  Feel only thy kiss

Voice of Infinity, sound in my heart, –
  Call of the One!
Stamp there thy radiance, never to part,
  O living Sun.[72]

Sri Aurobindo

THE MENTAL MIND

Mind and mentalisation

The "Mind" in the ordinary use of the word covers indiscriminately the whole consciousness, for man is a mental being and mentalises everything; but in the language of this yoga the words "mind" and "mental" are used to connote specially the part of the nature which *has to do** with cognition and intelligence, with ideas, with mental or thought perception, the reactions of thought to things, with the truly mental movements and formations, mental vision and will, etc., that are part of his intelligence.

... It is quite possible and even usual during a time shorter or longer, sometimes very long, for the mind to accept the Divine or the yogic ideal while the vital is unconvinced and unsurrendered and goes obstinately on its way of desire, passion and attraction to the ordinary life.[73]

Sri Aurobindo

The thought-mind

The proper function of the thought-mind is to observe, understand, judge with a dispassionate delight in knowledge and open itself to messages and illuminations playing upon all that it observes and upon all that is yet hidden from it but must progressively be revealed, messages and illuminations that secretly flash down to us from the divine Oracle concealed in light above our mentality whether they seem to descend through the intuitive mind or arise from the seeing heart.

---

* Emphasis ours. (Ed.)

But this it cannot do rightly because it is pinned to the limitations of the life-energy in the senses, to the discords of sensation and emotion, and to its own limitations of intellectual preference, inertia, straining, self-will which are the form taken in it by the interference of this desire-mind, this psychic Prana. As is said in the Upanishads, our whole mind-consciousness is shot through with the threads and currents of this Prana, this life-energy that strives and limits, grasps and misses, desires and suffers, and only by its purification can we know and possess our real and eternal self.[74]

Sri Aurobindo

The sensational thought-mind

This sensational thought-mind which is based upon sense, memory, association, first ideas and resultant generalisations or secondary ideas, is common to all developed animal life and mentality. Man indeed has given it an immense development and range and complexity impossible to the animal, but still, if he stopped there, he would only be a more highly effective animal. He gets beyond the animal range and height because he has been able to disengage and separate to a greater or less extent his thought action from the sense mentality, to draw back from the latter and observe its data and to act on it from above by a separated and partially freed intelligence. The intelligence and will of the animal are involved in the sense-mind and therefore altogether governed by it and carried on its stream of sensations, sense-perceptions, impulses; it is instinctive. Man is able to use a reason and will, a self-observing, thinking and all-observing, an intelligently willing mind which is no longer involved in the sense-mind, but acts from above and behind it in its own right, with a certain separateness and freedom. He is reflective, has a certain relative freedom of intelligent will. He has liberated in himself and has formed into a separate power the buddhi.[75]

Sri Aurobindo

*

... The movement of the Buddhi to exceed the limits of the sense-mind is an effort already half accomplished in the human evolution, it is part of the common operation of Nature in man.[76]

Sri Aurobindo

Pure intellectual understanding

By the understanding we mean that which at once perceives, judges and discriminates, the true reason of the human being not subservient to the senses, to desire or to the blind force of habit, but working in its own right for mastery, for knowledge. Certainly, the reason of man as he is at present does not even at its best act entirely in this free and sovereign fashion; but so far as it fails, it fails because it is still mixed with the lower half-animal action, because it is impure and constantly hampered and pulled down from its characteristic action. In its purity it should not be involved in these lower movements, but stand back from the object, and observe disinterestedly, put it in its right place in the whole by force of comparison, contrast, analogy, reason from its rightly observed data by deduction, induction, inference and holding all its gains in memory and supplementing them by a chastened and rightly-guided imagination view all in the light of a trained and disciplined judgment. Such is the pure intellectual understanding of which disinterested observation, judgment and reasoning are the law and characterising action.[77]

Sri Aurobindo

Understanding in the consciousness

If one has faith and openness that is enough. Besides there are two kinds of understanding – understanding by the intellect and understanding in the consciousness. It is good to have the former if it is accurate, but it is not indispensable. Understanding by the consciousness comes if there is faith and openness, though it may come only gradually and through steps of experience. But I have seen people without education or intellectuality understand in this way perfectly well the course of the yoga in themselves, while intellectual men make big mistakes, e.g. take a neutral mental quietude for the spiritual peace and refuse to come out of it in order to go further.[78]

Sri Aurobindo

The separation of the thinker and the thinking

In thought separation of the thinker and the thinking is more difficult. The thinker is plunged and lost in the thought or carried in the thought current, identified with it; it is not usually at the time of or in the very act of thinking that he can observe or review his thoughts, – he has to do that in retrospect and with the aid of memory or by a critical pause of corrective judgment before he proceeds further; but still a simultaneity of thinking and conscious direction of the mind's action can be achieved partially when the thought does not

The Mental Mind 85

engross, entirely when the thinker acquires the faculty of stepping back into the mental self and standing apart there from the mental energy. Instead of being absorbed in the thought with at most a vague feeling of the process of thinking, we can see the process by a mental vision, watch our thoughts in their origination and movement and, partly by a silent insight, partly by a process of thought upon thought, judge and evaluate them. But whatever the kind of identification, it is to be noted that the knowledge of our internal movements is of a double nature, separation and direct contact: for even when we detach ourselves, this close contact is maintained; our knowledge is always based on a direct touch, on a cognition by direct awareness carrying in it a certain element of identity. The more separative attitude is ordinarily the method of our reason in observing and knowing our inner movements; the more intimate is the method of our dynamic part of mind associating itself with our sensations, feelings and desires; but in this association too the thinking mind can intervene and exercise a separative dissociated observation and control over both the dynamic self-associating part of mind and the vital or physical movement. All the observable movements of our physical being also are known and controlled by us in both these ways, the separative and the intimate; we feel the body and what it is doing intimately as part of us, but the mind is separate from it and can exercise a detached control over its movements. This gives to our normal knowledge of our subjective being and nature, incomplete and largely superficial though it still is, yet, so far as it goes, a certain intimacy, immediacy and directness. That is absent in our knowledge of the world outside us and its movements and objects; for there, since the thing seen or experienced is not-self, not experienced as part of us, no entirely direct contact of consciousness with the object is possible; an instrumentation of sense has to be used which offers us, not immediate intimate knowledge of it, but a figure of it as a first datum for knowledge.[79]

Sri Aurobindo

Not mental control but control by the Divine Power

Once the vital being has come forward and shown its difficulty – there is nobody who has not one crucial difficulty or another there – it must be dealt with and conquered.

It must be dealt with not by the mind but directly by the supramental power.

Not peace and knowledge in the mind, but peace, faith, calm strength in the vital being itself (and especially in this part of it that is defective) is the thing to be established. To open yourself and allow all this to be brought down into it is the proper course.

The deficiency is not in the higher mind or mind proper; there is therefore no use in going back to establish mental peace. The difficulty is in that part of the vital being which is not sufficiently open and confident and not sufficiently strong and courageous and in the physical mind which lends its support to these things. To get the supramental light and calm and strength and intensity down there is what you need.

You may have all the mental knowledge in the world and yet be impotent to face vital difficulties. Courage, faith, sincerity towards the Light, rejection of opposite suggestions and adverse voices are there the true help. Then only can knowledge itself be at all effective.

Not mental control but some descent of a control from above the mind is the power demanded in the realisation. This control derived eventually from the supermind is a control by the Divine Power.[80]

Sri Aurobindo

The original action of the thought-mind

The original action of the thought-mind, the intelligence and will in man, is a subject action. It accepts the evidence of the senses, the commands of the life-cravings, instincts, desires, emotions, the impulses of the dynamic sense-mind and only tries to give them a more orderly direction and effective success. But the man whose reason and will are led and dominated by the lower mind, is an inferior type of human nature, and the part of our conscious being which consents to this domination is the lowest part of our manhood.[81]

Sri Aurobindo

Mind also is a half-light

And yet Mind also, our mentality, our thinking, understanding part, is not our Self, is not That, not the end or the beginning; it is a half-light thrown from the Infinite. The experience of mind as the creator of forms and things and of these forms and things existing in the Mind only, the thin subtle basis of idealism, is also a delusion, a half-view taken for the whole, a pale refracted light idealised as the burning body of the sun and its splendour. This idealist vision also does not arrive at the essence of being, does not even touch it but only an inferior mode of Nature. Mind is the dubious outer penumbra of a conscious existence which is not limited by mentality but exceeds it.[82]

Sri Aurobindo

Right thought

Still, right thought only becomes effective when in the purified understanding it is followed by other operations, by vision, by experience, by realisation.

What are these operations? They are not mere psychological self-analysis and self-observation. Such analysis, such observation are, like the process of right thought, of immense value and practically indispensable. They may even, if rightly pursued, lead to a right thought of considerable power and effectivity. Like intellectual discrimination by the process of meditative thought they will have an effect of purification; they will lead to self-knowledge of a certain kind and to the setting right of the disorders of the soul and the heart and even of the disorders of the understanding. Self-knowledge of all kinds is on the straight path to the knowledge of the real Self. The Upanishad tells us that the Self-existent has so set the doors of the soul that they turn outwards and most men look outward into the appearances of things; only the rare soul that is ripe for a calm thought and steady wisdom turns its eye inward, sees the Self and attains to immortality. To this turning of the eye inward psychological self-observation and analysis is a great and effective introduction. We can look into the inward of ourselves more easily than we can look into the inward of things external to us because there, in things outside us, we are in the first place embarrassed by the form and secondly we have no natural previous experience of that in them which is other than their physical substance. A purified or tranquillised mind may reflect or a powerful concentration may discover God in the world, the Self in Nature even before it is realised in ourselves, but this is rare and difficult*. And it is only in ourselves that we can observe and know the process of the self in its becoming and follow the process by which it draws back into self-being. Therefore the ancient counsel, know thyself, will always stand as the first word that directs us towards *the* knowledge. Still, psychological self-knowledge is only the experience of the modes of the Self, it is not the realisation of the Self in its pure being.[83]

Sri Aurobindo

---

* In one respect, however, it is easier, because in external things we are not so much hampered by the sense of the limited ego as in ourselves; one obstacle to the realisation of God is therefore removed.

Mind is a delusion

Then suddenly a luminous finger fell
On all things seen or touched or heard or felt
And showed his mind that nothing could be known;
That must be reached from which all knowledge comes.
The sceptic Ray disrupted all that seems
And smote at the very roots of thought and sense.
In a universe of Nescience they have grown,
Aspiring towards a superconscient Sun,
Playing in shine and rain from heavenlier skies
They never can win however high their reach
Or overpass however keen their probe.
A doubt corroded even the means to think,
Distrust was thrown upon Mind's instruments;
All that it takes for reality's shining coin,
Proved fact, fixed inference, deduction clear,
Firm theory, assured significance,
Appeared as frauds upon Time's credit bank
Or assets valueless in Truth's treasury.
An Ignorance on an uneasy throne
Travestied with a fortuitous sovereignty
A figure of knowledge garbed in dubious words
And tinsel thought-forms brightly inadequate.
A labourer in the dark dazzled by half-light,
What it knew was an image in a broken glass,
What it saw was real but its sight untrue.
All the ideas in its vast repertory
Were like the mutterings of a transient cloud
That spent itself in sound and left no trace.[84]

Sri Aurobindo

The ego-mind

Self-will in thought and action has, we have already seen, to be quite renounced if we would be perfect in the way of divine works; it has equally to be renounced if we are to be perfect in divine knowledge. This self-will means an egoism in the mind which attaches itself to its preferences, its habits, its past or present formations of thought and view and will because it regards them as itself or its own, weaves around them the delicate threads of "I-ness" and "my-ness" and lives in them like a spider in its web. It hates to be disturbed, as a spider hates attack on its web, and feels foreign and unhappy if transplanted to fresh viewpoints and formations as a spider feels foreign in another web than its own. This attachment must be entirely excised from the mind. Not only must we give up the ordinary attitude to the world and life to which the unawakened mind clings as its natural element; but we must not remain bound in any mental construction of our own or in any intellectual thought-system or arrangement of religious dogmas or logical conclusion; we must not only cut asunder the snare of the mind and the senses, but flee also beyond the snare of the thinker, the snare of the theologian and the church-builder, the meshes of the Word and the bondage of the Idea. All these are within us waiting to wall in the spirit with forms; but we must always go beyond, always renounce the lesser for the greater, the finite for the Infinite; we must be prepared to proceed from illumination to illumination, from experience to experience, from soul-state to soul-state so as to reach the utmost transcendence of the Divine and its utmost universality. Nor must we attach ourselves even to the truths we hold most securely, for they are but forms and expressions of the Ineffable who refuses to limit himself to any form or expression; always we must keep ourselves open to the higher Word from above that does not confine itself to its own sense and the light of the Thought that carries in it its own opposites.

But the centre of all resistance is egoism and this we must pursue into every covert and disguise and drag it out and slay it; for its disguises are endless and it will cling to every shred of possible self-concealment.[85]

Sri Aurobindo

Our mind is a house haunted by the slain past

Our mind is a house haunted by the slain past,
Ideas soon mummified, ghosts of old truths,
God's spontaneities tied with formal strings
And packed into drawers of reason's trim bureau,
A grave of great lost opportunities,
Or an office for misuse of soul and life
And all the waste man makes of heaven's gifts
And all his squanderings of Nature's store,
A stage for the comedy of Ignorance.[86]

Sri Aurobindo

Our real self

For our real self is not the individual mental being, that is only a figure, an appearance; our real self is cosmic, infinite, it is one with all existence and the inhabitant of all existences. The self behind our mind, life and body is the same as the self behind the mind, life and body of all our fellow-beings, and if we come to possess it, we shall naturally, when we turn to look out again upon them, tend to become one with them in the common basis of our consciousness. It is true that the mind opposes any such identification and if we allow it to persist in its old habits and activities, it will rather strive to bring again its veil of dissonances over our new realisation and possession of self than to shape and subject itself to this true and eternal vision of things. But in the first place, if we have proceeded rightly on the path of our Yoga, we shall have attained to Self through a purified mind and heart, and a purified mind is one that is necessarily passive and open to the knowledge. Secondly, even the mind in spite of its tendency to limit and divide can be taught to think in the rhythm of the unifying Truth instead of the broken terms of the limiting appearance. We must therefore accustom it by meditation and concentration to cease to think of things and beings as separately existent in themselves and rather to think always of the One everywhere and of all things as the One. Although we have spoken hitherto of the withdrawing motion of the Jiva as the first necessity of knowledge and as if it were to be pursued alone and by itself, yet in fact it is better for the Sadhaka of the integral Yoga to unite the two movements. By one he will find the self within, by the other he will find that self in all that seems to us at present to be outside us. It is possible indeed to begin with the latter movement, to realise all things in this visible and sensible existence as God or Brahman or Virat Purusha and then to go beyond to all that is behind the Virat. But this has its inconveniences and it is better, if that be found possible, to combine the two movements.[87]

Sri Aurobindo

Essential mentality is idealistic

The mental life concentrates on the aesthetic, the ethical and the intellectual activities. Essential mentality is idealistic and a seeker after perfection. The subtle self, the brilliant Atman*, is ever a dreamer. A dream of perfect beauty, perfect conduct, perfect Truth, whether seeking new forms of the Eternal or revitalising the old, is the very soul of pure mentality. But it knows not how to deal with the resistance of Matter. There it is hampered and inefficient, works by bungling experiments and has either to withdraw from the struggle or submit to the grey actuality. Or else, by studying the material life and accepting the conditions of the contest, it may succeed, but only in imposing temporarily some artificial system which infinite Nature either rends and casts aside or disfigures out of recognition or by withdrawing her assent leaves as the corpse of a dead ideal. Few and far between have been those realisations of the dreamer in Man which the world has gladly accepted, looks back to with a fond memory and seeks, in its elements, to cherish.[88]

Sri Aurobindo

---

* Who dwells in Dream, the inly conscious, the enjoyer of abstractions, the Brilliant. *Mandukya Upanishad*, 4.

This witness hush is the Thinker's secret base

His mind reflected this vast quietism.
This witness hush is the thinker's secret base:
Hidden in silent depths the word is formed,
From hidden silences the act is born
Into the voiceful mind, the labouring world;
In secrecy wraps the seed the Eternal sows
Silence, the mystic birthplace of the soul.
In God's supreme withdrawn and timeless hush
A seeing Self and potent Energy met;
The Silence knew itself and thought took form:
Self-made from the dual power creation rose.
In the still self he lived and it in him;
Its mute immemorable listening depths,
Its vastness and its stillness were his own;
One being with it he grew wide, powerful, free.
Apart, unbound, he looked on all things done.
As one who builds his own imagined scenes
And loses not himself in what he sees,
Spectator of a drama self-conceived,
He looked on the world and watched its motive thoughts
With the burden of luminous prophecy in their eyes,
Its forces with their feet of wind and fire
Arisen from the dumbness in his soul.
All now he seemed to understand and know;
Desire came not nor any gust of will,
The great perturbed inquirer lost his task;
Nothing was asked nor wanted any more.
There he could stay, the Self, the Silence won:
His soul had peace, it knew the cosmic Whole.[89]

Sri Aurobindo

Silence and the knowledge of the Self

But for the knowledge of the Self it is necessary to have the power of a complete intellectual passivity, the power of dismissing all thought, the power of the mind to think not at all which the Gita in one passage enjoins. This is a hard saying for the occidental mind to which thought is the highest thing and which will be apt to mistake the power of the mind not to think, its complete silence for the incapacity of thought. But this power of silence is a capacity and not an incapacity, a power and not a weakness. It is a profound and pregnant stillness. Only when the mind is thus entirely still, like clear, motionless and level water, in a perfect purity and peace of the whole being and the soul transcends thought, can the Self which exceeds and originates all activities and becomings, the Silence from which all words are born, the Absolute of which all relativities are partial reflections manifest itself in the pure essence of our being. In a complete silence only is the Silence heard; in a pure peace only is its Being revealed. Therefore to us the name of That is the Silence and the Peace.[90]

Sri Aurobindo

Constant silence in the mind

If you open to the higher regions of consciousness and the force descends from above, quite naturally it establishes a silence in the lower regions, for they are governed by this higher power which descends. This comes from higher regions of the mind or from beyond, even from the supermind. So when this force and consciousness come down and enter into the consciousness of a lower plane, this consciousness becomes naturally quiet, for it is as though invaded, flooded by that higher light which transforms it.

In fact, this is even the only way of establishing a constant silence in one's mind. It is to open oneself to higher regions and let this higher consciousness, force, light descend constantly into the lower mind and take possession of it. And here, when this happens, the lower mind can remain constantly quiet and silent, because it is this one which acts and fills the whole being. One can act, write and speak without the mind being active, with this force which comes from above penetrating the mind and using it; and the mind itself becomes just a passive instrument. And in fact, this is the only way of establishing silence; for once this is established, the silence is established, the mind cannot stir any longer, it acts only under the impulsion of this force when it manifests in it. It is like a very quiet, very silent field and the force when it comes puts the elements into movement and uses them, and it finds expression through the mind without the mind being agitated. It remains very quiet.[91]

The Mother

The mind has to be quiet during an experience

That is always the difficulty with the mind. It must learn to be silent and let the knowledge come without trying to catch hold of it for its own play.[92]

*

During the experience the mind should be quiet. After the experience is over it can be active. If it is active while it is there, the experience may stop altogether.[93]

*

The Mental Mind

To think and question about an experience when it is happening is the wrong thing to do; it stops it or diminishes it. Let the experience have its full play – if it is something like this "new life force" or peace or Force or anything else helpful. When it is over, you can think about it – not while it is proceeding. For these experiences are spiritual and not mental and the mind has to be quiet and not interfere.[94]

Sri Aurobindo

The spectator and creator Mind

This great spectator and creator Mind
Was only some half-seeing's delegate,
A veil that hung between the soul and Light,
An idol, not the living body of God.
Even the still spirit that looks upon its works
Was some pale front of the Unknowable;
A shadow seemed the wide and witness Self,
Its liberation and immobile calm
A void recoil of being from Time-made things,
Not the self-vision of Eternity.
Deep peace was there, but not the nameless Force:
Our sweet and mighty Mother was not there
Who gathers to her bosom her children's lives,
Her clasp that takes the world into her arms
In the fathomless rapture of the Infinite,
The Bliss that is creation's splendid grain
Or the white passion of God-ecstasy
That laughs in the blaze of the boundless heart of Love.
A greater Spirit than the Self of Mind
Must answer to the questioning of his soul.[95]

Sri Aurobindo

Knowledge is not Wisdom

A burden of transient gains weighs down her steps
And hardly under that load can she advance;
But the hours cry to her, she travels on
Passing from thought to thought, from want to want;
Her greatest progress is a deepened need.
Matter dissatisfies, she turns to Mind;
She conquers earth, her field, then claims the heavens.
Insensible, breaking the work she has done
The stumbling ages over her labour pass,
But still no great transforming light came down
And no revealing rapture touched her fall.
Only a glimmer sometimes splits mind's sky
Justifying the ambiguous providence
That makes of night a path to unknown dawns
Or a dark clue to some diviner state.
In Nescience began her mighty task,
In Ignorance she pursues the unfinished work,
For knowledge gropes, but meets not Wisdom's face.
Ascending slowly with unconscious steps,
A foundling of the Gods she wanders here
Like a child-soul left near the gates of Hell
Fumbling through fog in search of Paradise.[96]

Sri Aurobindo

Rightly to know and express the Highest

But rightly to know and express the Highest is not easy for man the mental being because the highest Truth and therefore the highest modes of existence are supramental. They repose on the essential unity of what seem to the intellect and mind and are to our mental experience of the world opposite poles of existence and idea and therefore irreconcilable opposites and contradictions, but to the supramental experience are complementary aspects of the same Truth. We have seen this already in the necessity of realising the Self as at once one and many; for we have to realise each thing and being as That; we have to realise the unity of all as That, both in the unity of sum and in the oneness of essence; and we have to realise That as the Transcendent who is beyond all this unity and this multiplicity which we see everywhere as the two opposite, yet companion poles of all existence. For every individual being is the Self, the Divine in spite of the outward limitations of the mental and physical form through which it presents itself at the actual moment, in the actual field of space, in the actual succession of circumstances that make up the web of inner state and outward action and event through which we know the individual. So, equally, every collectivity small or great is each the Self, the Divine similarly expressing itself in the conditions of this manifestation. We cannot really know any individual or any collectivity if we know it only as it appears inwardly to itself or outwardly to us, but only if we know it as the Divine, the One, our own Self employing its various essential modes and its occasional circumstances of self-manifestation. Until we have transformed the habits of our mentality so that it shall live entirely in this knowledge reconciling all differences in the One, we do not live in the real Truth, because we do not live in the real Unity. The accomplished sense of Unity is not that in which all are regarded as parts of one whole, waves of one sea, but that in which each as well as the All is regarded wholly as the Divine, wholly as our Self in a supreme identity.[97]

Sri Aurobindo

The final realisation

This Self that we are has finally to become to our self-consciousness entirely one with all existences in spite of its exceeding them. We have to see it not only as that which contains and inhabits all, but that which is all, not only as indwelling spirit, but also as the name and form, the movement and the master of the movement, the mind and life and body. It is by this final realisation that we shall resume entirely in the right poise and the vision of the Truth all that we drew back from in the first movement of recoil and withdrawal. The individual mind, life and body which we recoiled from as not our true being, we shall recover as a true becoming of the Self, but no longer in a purely individual narrowness. We shall take up the mind not as a separate mentality imprisoned in a petty motion, but as a large movement of the universal mind, the life not as an egoistic activity of vitality and sensation and desire, but as a free movement of the universal life, the body not as a physical prison of the soul but as a subordinate instrument and detachable robe, realising that also as a movement of universal Matter, a cell of the cosmic Body. We shall come to feel all the consciousness of the physical world as one with our physical consciousness, feel all the energies of the cosmic life around as our own energies, feel all the heart-beats of the great cosmic impulse and seeking in our heart-beats set to the rhythm of the divine Ananda, feel all the action of the universal mind flowing into our mentality and our thought-action flowing out upon it as a wave into that wide sea. This unity embracing all mind, life and matter in the light of a supramental Truth and the pulse of a spiritual Bliss will be to us our internal fulfilment of the Divine in a complete cosmic consciousness.[98]

Sri Aurobindo

THE PSYCHIC MIND

The word psychic

Ordinarily, all the more inward and all the abnormal psychological experiences are called psychic. I use the word psychic for the soul as distinguished from the mind and vital. All movements and experiences of the soul would in that sense be called psychic, those which rise from or directly touch the psychic being; where mind and vital predominate, the experience would be called psychological (surface or occult). "Spiritual" has not a necessary connection with the Absolute. Of course the experience of the Absolute is spiritual. All contacts with self, the higher consciousness, the Divine above are spiritual. There are others that could not be so sharply classified or one set off against another.

The spiritual realisation is of primary importance and indispensable. I would consider it best to have the spiritual and psychic development first and have it with the same fullness before entering the occult regions. Those who enter the latter first may find their spiritual realisation much delayed – others fall into the mazy traps of the occult and do not come out in this life. Some no doubt can carry on both together, the occult and the spiritual, and make them help each other; but the process I suggest is the safer.

The governing factors for us must be the spirit and the psychic being united with the Divine – the occult laws and phenomena have to be known but only as an instrumentation, not as the governing principles. The occult is a vast field and complicated and not without its dangers. It need not be abandoned but it should not be given the first place.[99]

Sri Aurobindo

The word psychic is indeed used in English to indicate anything that is other or deeper than the external mind, life and body or it indicates sometimes anything occult or supraphysical; but that is a use which brings confusion and error and we have almost entirely to discard it.[100]

Sri Aurobindo

Psychic mind and mental psychic

Psychic mind and mental psychic are the same thing practically – when there is a movement of the mind in which the psychic influence predominates, it is called the psychic in the mind or the psychic mind.[101]

Sri Aurobindo

*

When the mind is turned towards the Divine and the Truth and feels and responds to that only or mainly, it can be called a psychic mind – it is something formed by the influence of the psychic being on the mental plane.[102]

Sri Aurobindo

*

There is always a part of the mind, of the vital, of the body which is or can be influenced by the psychic; they can be called the psychic-mental, the psychic-vital, the psychic-physical. According to the personality or the degree of evolution of each person, this part can be small or large, weak or strong, covered up and inactive or prominent and in action. When it acts the movements of the mind, vital or physical accept the psychic motives or aims, partake of the nature of the psychic or follow its aims but with a modification in the manner which belongs to the mind, vital or physical. The psychic-vital seeks after the Divine, but it has a demand in its self-giving, desire, vital eagerness. The psychic has not, for the psychic has instead pure self-giving, aspiration, intensity of psychic fire. The psychic-vital is subject to pain and suffering, which there is not in the psychic.[103]

Sri Aurobindo

Nature of the psychic

Your idea of psychic is certainly a mental construction which should be avoided. The psychic has indeed the quality of peace – but that is not its main character as it is of the Self or Atman. The psychic is the divine element in the individual being and its characteristic power is to turn everything towards the Divine, to bring a fire of purification, aspiration, devotion, true light of discernment, feeling, will, an action which transforms by degrees the whole nature. Quietude, peace and silence in the heart and therefore in the vital part of the being are necessary to reach the psychic, to plunge in it, for the perturbations of the vital nature, desire, emotion turned ego-wards or world-wards are the main part of the screen that hides the soul from the nature. It is better, therefore, to be free from the mental constructions when you take the plunge and to have only the sense of aspiration, of devotion, of self-giving to the Divine.[104]

Sri Aurobindo

The mind and the psychic being

The chief obstacle in you is the mind. If you can quiet the mind and give the psychic being a chance, that will be your spiritual salvation. Your mind is inordinately active, too full of questionings, too shrewd, worldly and practical, too much given to doubt and self-defence. All that is very useful in worldly life, it helps to bring success, but it is not the way to succeed in Yoga. No doubt in Yoga, the critical rational mind (self-critical as well as critical of things outside you) is an element that has its value so long as the true inner discrimination does not come; but of itself it cannot carry you on the way, it will only make your progress slow and stumbling. There must be something in you that will open itself directly to the Truth and the Light. The unregenerated vital being of man cannot do that because it demands of the higher power that it shall satisfy the vital desires, demands, ambitions, vanity, pride etc., before it will accept the Truth. The unillumined mind also cannot do it because it refuses to recognise the Truth unless the Truth first satisfied its own judgments, ideas, opinions, critical or conventional standards, – unless in a word the Truth consents to narrow itself into the moulds of the mind's own ignorance. It is the psychic being alone that turns to the Truth directly, feels it instinctively behind all appearances and in spite of all disguises, accepts it without any egoistic demand or condition, is ready to serve it without reserve or refusal. It is the psychic being also that can at once feel and reject all imitations of the Truth, all shows, all pretences.[105]

Sri Aurobindo

Soul and psychic being

The soul is something of the Divine that descends into the evolution as a divine Principle within it to support the evolution of the individual out of the Ignorance into the Light. It develops in the course of the evolution a psychic individual or soul individuality which grows from life to life, using the evolving mind, vital and body as its instruments. It is the soul that is immortal while the rest disintegrates; it passes from life to life carrying its experience in essence and the continuity of the evolution of the individual.[106]

Sri Aurobindo

*

The soul is a spark of the Divine which is not seated above the manifested being, but comes down into the manifestation to support its evolution in the material world. It is at first an undifferentiated power of the Divine Consciousness containing all possibilities which have not yet taken form, but to which it is the function of evolution to give form. This spark is there in all living beings from the lowest to the highest.

The psychic being is formed by the soul in its evolution. It supports the mind, vital, body, grows by their experiences, carries the nature from life to life. It is the psychic or *chaitya puruṣa*. At first it is veiled by mind, vital and body, but as it grows, it becomes capable of coming forward and dominating the mind, life and body; in the ordinary man it depends on them for expression and is not able to take them up and freely use them. The life of the being is animal or human and not divine. When the psychic being can by sadhana become dominant and freely use its instruments, then the impulse towards the Divine becomes complete and the transformation of mind, vital and body, not merely their liberation, becomes possible.[107]

Sri Aurobindo

*

The soul and the psychic being are practically the same, except that even in things which have not developed a psychic being, there is still a spark of the Divine which can be called the soul. The psychic being is called in Sanskrit the Purusha in the heart or the Chaitya Purusha. (The psychic being is the soul developing in the evolution.)[108]

Sri Aurobindo

*

It is this secret psychic entity which is the true original Conscience in us deeper than the constructed and conventional conscience of the moralist, for it is this which points always towards Truth and Right and Beauty, towards Love and Harmony and all that is a divine possibility in us, and persists till these things become the major need of our nature. It is the psychic personality in us that flowers as the saint, the sage, the seer; when it reaches its full strength, it turns the being towards the Knowledge of Self and the Divine, towards the supreme Truth, the supreme Good, the supreme Beauty, Love and Bliss, the divine heights and largenesses, and opens us to the touch of spiritual sympathy, universality, oneness.[109]

Sri Aurobindo

The Psychic Mind

The true soul secret in us.... This veiled psychic entity is the flame of the Godhead always alight within us, inextinguishable even by that dense unconsciousness of any spiritual self within which obscures our outward nature. It is a flame born out of the Divine and, luminous inhabitant of the Ignorance, grows in it till it is able to turn it towards the Knowledge. It is the concealed Witness and Control, the hidden Guide, the Daemon of Socrates, the inner light or inner voice of the mystic. It is that which endures and is imperishable in us from birth to birth, untouched by death, decay or corruption, an indestructible spark of the Divine. Not the unborn Self or Atman.... It is yet its deputy in the forms of Nature, the individual soul, *caitya puruṣa*, supporting mind, life and body, standing behind the mental, the vital the subtle-physical. Being in us and watching and profiting by their development and experience.[110]

Sri Aurobindo

The inner consciousness and the psychic being

The inner consciousness means the inner mind, inner vital, inner physical and behind them the psychic which is their inmost being. But the inner mind is not the higher mind; it is more in touch with the universal forces and more open to the higher consciousness and capable of an immensely deeper and larger range of action than the outer or surface mind – but it is of the same essential nature. The higher consciousness is that above the ordinary mind and different from it in its workings; it ranges from higher mind through illumined mind, intuition and overmind up to the border line of the supramental.

If the psychic were liberated, free to act in its own way,

there would not be all this stumbling in the ignorance. But the psychic is covered up by the ignorant mind, vital and physical and compelled to act through them according to the law of the Ignorance. If it is liberated from this covering, then it can act according to its own nature with a free aspiration, a direct contact with the higher consciousness and a power to change the ignorant nature.[111]

Sri Aurobindo

*

The true being mental, vital or subtle physical has always the greater qualities of its plane – it is the Purusha and like the psychic, though in another way, the projection of the Divine, therefore in connection with the higher consciousness and reflects something of it, though it is not altogether that – it is also in tune with the cosmic Truth.[112]

Sri Aurobindo

The psychic in little children

This little true thing in the child is the divine Presence in the psychic – it is also there in plants and animals. In plants it is not conscious, in animals it begins to be conscious, and in children it is very conscious. I have known children who were much more conscious of their psychic being at the age of five than at fourteen, and at fourteen than at twenty-five; and above all, from the moment they go to school where they undergo that kind of intensive mental training which draws their attention to the intellectual part of their being, they lose almost always and almost completely this contact with their psychic being.

... Look carefully... into the eyes of little children, and you will see a kind of light – some describe it as frank – but so true, so true, which looks at the world with wonder. Well, this sense of wonder, it is the wonder of the psychic which sees the truth but does not understand much about the world, for it is too far from it. Children have this but as they learn more, become more intelligent, more educated, this is effaced, and you see all sorts of things in their eyes: thoughts, desires, passions, wickedness – but this kind of little flame, so pure, is no longer there. And you may be sure it is the mind that has got in there, and the psychic has gone very far behind.[113]

The Mother

The right object of education

It is not yet realised what this soul is or that the true secret, whether with child or man, is to help him to find his deeper self, the real psychic entity within. That, if we ever give it a chance to come forward, still more if we call it into the foreground as "the leader of the march set in our front", will itself take up most of the business of education out of our hands and develop the capacity of the psychological being towards a realisation of its potentialities of which our present mechanical view of life and man and external routine methods of dealing with them prevent us from having any experience or forming any conception. These new educational methods are on the straight way to this truer dealing. The closer touch attempted with the psychical entity behind the vital and physical mentality and an increasing reliance on its possibilities must lead to the ultimate discovery that man is inwardly a soul and a conscious power of the Divine and that the evocation of this real man within is *the right object of education** and indeed of all human life if it would find and live according to the hidden Truth and deepest law of its own being. That was the knowledge which the ancients sought to express through religious and social symbolism, and subjectivism is a road of return to the lost knowledge. First deepening man's inner experience, restoring perhaps on an unprecedented scale insight and self-knowledge to the race, it must end by revolutionising his social and collective self-expression.**[114]

Sri Aurobindo

The psychic is the solution

This danger of [the human confusion of values] can only be countered by the opening of a now nine-tenths concealed inmost soul or psychic being that is already there but not commonly active within us. That is the inner light we must liberate; for the light of this inmost soul is our one sure illumination so long as we walk still amidst the siege of the Ignorance and the Truth-consciousness has not taken up the entire control of our Godward endeavour. The working of the Divine Force in us under the conditions of the transition and the light of the psychic being turning us always towards a conscious and seeing obedience to that higher impulsion and away from the demands and instigations of the Forces of the Ignorance, these between them create an ever progressive inner law of our action which continues till the spiritual

---

* Emphasis ours. (Ed.)

** On the psychic being itself see the compilation by A.S. Dalal entitled: *The psychic being.*

The Psychic Mind

and supramental can be established in our nature. In the transition there may well be a period in which we take up all life and action and offer them to the Divine for purification, change and deliverance of the truth within them, another period in which we draw back and build a spiritual wall around us admitting through its gates only such activities as consent to undergo the law of the spiritual transformation, a third in which a free and all-embracing action, but with new forms fit for the utter truth of the Spirit, can again be made possible. These things, however, will be decided by no mental rule but in the light of the soul within us and by the ordaining force and progressive guidance of the Divine Power that secretly or overtly first impels, then begins clearly to control and order and finally takes up the whole burden of the Yoga.[115]

Sri Aurobindo

The psychic and the other parts of the being

In every human being there are two parts, the psychic with so much of the thinking mind and higher (emotional, larger dynamic) vital that is open to the psychic and cleaves to the soul's aims and admits the higher experiences and on the other hand the lower vital and the physical or external being (external mind and vital included) which are attached to the ignorant personality and nature and do not want to change. It is the conflict between these two that makes all the difficulty of the sadhana. All the difficulties you enumerate arise from that and nothing else. It is only by curing the duality that one can overcome them. That happens when one is able to live within, aware of one's inner being, identified with it and to regard the rest as not oneself, as a creation of ignorant Nature from which one has separated oneself and which has to disappear and, secondly, when by opening oneself constantly to the Divine Light and Force and the Mother's presence a dynamic action of sadhana is constantly maintained which steadily pushes out the movements of the ignorance and substitutes even in the lower vital and physical being the movements of the inner and higher nature. There is then no struggle any longer, but an automatic growth of the divine elements and fading out of the undivine. The devotion of the heart, and the increasing activity of the psychic being, which is best helped by devotion and self-giving, are the most powerful means for arriving at this condition.[116]

Sri Aurobindo

Identification of the soul with mind

Nature has created within her mental unity, formed in the universal Mind separate-seeming dynamos as it were of mentality, constant centres for the generation, distribution and reabsorption of mental force and mental activities, stations as it were in a system of mental telegraphy where messages are conceived, written, sent, received, deciphered, and these messages and these activities are of many kinds, sensational, emotional, perceptual, conceptual, intuitional, all of which the Soul manifested in mental Nature accepts, uses for its outlook on the world and seems to itself to project and to receive their shocks, to suffer or to master their consequences. Nature installs the base of these dynamos in the material bodies she has formed, makes these bodies the ground for her stations and connects the mental with the material by a nerve-system full of the movement of vital currents through which the mind becomes conscious of the material world and, so far as it chooses, of the vital world of nature. Otherwise the mind would be conscious of the mental world first and chiefly and would only indirectly glimpse the material. As it is, its attention is fixed on the body and the material world in which it has been installed and it is aware of the rest of existence only dimly, indirectly or subconsciously in that vast remainder of itself with regard to which superficially it has become irresponsive and oblivious.

The Soul identifies itself with this mental dynamo or station and says "I am this mind". And since the mind is absorbed in the bodily life, it thinks "I am a mind in a living body" or, still more commonly, "I am a body which lives and thinks". It identifies itself with the thoughts, emotions, sensations of the embodied mind and imagines that because when the body is dissolved all this will dissolve, itself also will cease to exist. Or if it becomes conscious of the current of persistence of mental personality, it thinks of itself as a mental soul occupying the body whether once or repeatedly and returning from earthly living to mental worlds beyond; the persistence of this mental being mentally enjoying or suffering sometimes in the body, sometimes on the mental or vital plane of Nature it calls its immortal existence. Or else, because the mind is a principle of light and knowledge, however imperfect, and can have some notion of what is beyond it, it sees the possibility of a dissolution of the mental being into that which is beyond, some Void or some eternal Existence, and it says, "There I, the mental soul, cease to be". Such dissolution it dreads or desires, denies or affirms according to its measure of attachment to or repulsion from this present play of embodied mind and vitality.

Now, all this is a mixture of truth and falsehood. Mind, Life, Matter exist and mental, vital, physical individualisation exists as facts in Nature, but the identification of the soul with these things is a false identification. Mind, Life and Matter are ourselves only in this sense that they are principles of being which the true self has evolved by the meeting and interaction of Soul and Nature in order to express a form of its one existence as the Cosmos.... Individual mind, life and body are forms of ourselves in so far as we are centres of the multiplicity of the One; universal Mind, Life and Body are also forms of our self, because we are that One in our being. But the self is more than universal or individual mind, life and body and when we limit ourselves by identification with these things, we found our knowledge on a falsehood, we falsify our determining view and our practical experience not only of our self-being but of our cosmic existence and of our individual activities.

The Self is an eternal utter being and pure existence of *which all these things are becomings**. From this knowledge we have to proceed; this knowledge we have to realise and make it the foundation of the inner and the outer life of the individual.[117]

Sri Aurobindo

Emergence of the soul as distinct from mind

So too at first soul in man does not appear as something quite distinct from mind and from mentalised life; its movements are involved in the mind-movements, its operation seem to be mental and emotional activities; the mental human being is not aware of a soul in him standing back from the mind and life and body, detaching itself, seeing and controlling and moulding their action and formation; but, as the inner

---

* Emphasis ours. (Ed.)

The Psychic Mind

evolution proceeds, this is precisely what can, must and does happen, – it is the long-delayed but inevitable next step in our evolutionary destiny. There can be a decisive emergence in which the being separates itself from thought and sees itself in an inner silence as the spirit in mind, or separates itself from the life-movements, desires, sensations, kinetic impulses and is aware of itself as *the spirit supporting life**, or separates itself from the body-sense and knows itself as a spirit ensouling Matter: this is the discovery of ourselves as the Purusha, a mental being or a life-soul or a subtle self supporting the body.... But self-discovery can go farther, it can even put aside all relation to form or action of Nature. For it is seen that these selves are representations of a divine Entity to which mind, life and body are only forms and instruments: we are then the Soul looking at Nature, knowing all her dynamisms in us, not by mental perception and observation, but by an intrinsic consciousness and its direct sense of things and its intimate exact vision, able therefore by its emergence to put a close control on our nature and change it. When there is a complete silence in the being, either a stillness of the whole being or a stillness behind unaffected by surface movements, then we can become aware of a Self, a spiritual substance of our being, an existence exceeding even the soul-individuality, spreading itself into universality, surpassing all dependence on any natural form or action, extending itself upward into a transcendence of which the limits are not visible. It is these liberations of the spiritual part in us which are the decisive steps of the spiritual evolution in nature.[118]

Sri Aurobindo

* Emphasis ours. (Ed.)

Self-consecration from the mind to the inner being

But in whatever way it comes, there must be a decision of the mind and the will and, as its result, a complete and effective self-consecration. The acceptance of a new spiritual idea-force and upward orientation in the being, an illumination, a turning or conversion seized on by the will and the heart's aspiration, – this is the momentous act which contains as in a seed all the results that the Yoga has to give. The mere idea or intellectual seeking of something higher beyond, however strongly grasped by the mind's interest, is ineffective unless it is seized on by the heart as the one thing desirable and by the will as the one thing to be done. For truth of the Spirit has not to be merely thought but to be lived, and to live it demands a unified single-mindedness of the being; so great a change as is contemplated by the Yoga is not to be effected by a divided will or by a small portion of the energy or by a hesitating mind. He who seeks the Divine must consecrate himself to God and to God only.

If the change comes suddenly and decisively by an overpowering influence, there is no further essential or lasting difficulty. The choice follows upon the thought, or is simultaneous with it, and the self-consecration follows upon the choice. The feet are already set upon the path, even if they seem at first to wander uncertainly and even though the path itself may be only obscurely seen and the knowledge of the goal may be imperfect. The secret Teacher, the inner Guide is already at work, though he may not yet manifest himself or may not yet appear in the person of his human representative. Whatever difficulties and hesitations may ensue, they cannot eventually prevail against the power of the experience that has turned the current of the life. The call, once decisive, stands; the thing that has been born cannot eventually be stifled. Even if the force of circumstances prevents a regular pursuit or a full practical self-consecration from the first, still the mind has taken its bent and persists and returns with an ever-increasing effect upon its leading preoccupation. There is an ineluctable persistence of the inner being, and against it circumstances are in the end powerless, and no weakness in the nature can for long be an obstacle.[119]

Sri Aurobindo

Thoughts of the outer mind and psychic thoughts

I did not quite understand from your letter what is the nature of these sights and objects that pass like a cinema film before you. If they are things seen by the inner vision, then there is no need to drive them away – one has only to let them pass. When one does sadhana an inner mind which is within us awakes and sees by an inner vision images of all things in this world and other worlds – this power of vision has its use, though one has not to be attached to it; one can let them pass with a quiet mind, neither fixing on them not driving them away. It is the thoughts of the outer mind that have to be refused, the suggestions and ideas that end by disturbing the sadhana. There are also a number of thoughts of all kinds that have no interest, but which the mind was accustomed to allow to come as a habit, mechanically, – these sometimes come up when one tries to be quiet. They must be allowed to pass away without attending to them until they run down and the mind becomes still; to struggle with them and try to stop them is no use, there must be only a quiet rejection. On the other hand if thoughts come up from within, from the psychic, thoughts of the Mother, of divine love and joy, perceptions of truth etc., these of course must be permitted, as they help to make the psychic active.[120]

Sri Aurobindo

Psychic growth and usefulness of the mind

Psychic life in the universe is a work of the divine Grace. Psychic growth is a work of the divine Grace and the ultimate power of the psychic being over the physical being will also be a result of the divine Grace. And the mind, if it wants to be at all useful, has only to remain very quiet, as quiet as it can, because if it meddles in it, it is sure to spoil everything.

So there will be no need of the mind?

Ah, excuse me, I did not say that one doesn't need the mind. The mind is useful for something else. The mind is an instrument for formation and organisation, and if the mind lets the psychic make use of it, that will be very good. But it is not the mind which will help the psychic to manifest. The roles are reversed. The mind can be an instrument for the manifestation of the psychic later, when it has already taken possession of the outer consciousness. It is rarely so before that. Usually it is a veil and an obstruction. But surely it can't help in the manifestation. It can help in the action if it takes its true place and true movement. And if it becomes completely docile to the psychic inspiration, it can help to organise life, for this is its function, its reason of existence. But first of all the psychic must have taken possession of the field, must be the master of the house. Then, later, things can be arranged.[121]

The Mother

THE SPIRITUAL MIND

The spiritual mind

The spiritual mind is a mind which, in its fullness, is aware of the Self, reflecting the Divine, seeing and understanding the nature of the Self and its relations with the manifestation, living in that or in contact with it, calm, wide and awake to higher knowledge, not perturbed by the play of the forces. When it gets its full liberated movement, its central station is very usually felt above the head, though its influence can extend downward through all the being and outward through space.[122]

*

Higher Mind is one of the planes of the spiritual mind, the first and lowest of them; it is above the normal mental level.[123]

Sri Aurobindo

*

The sage and seer live in the spiritual mind, their thought or their vision is governed and moulded by an inner or a greater divine light of knowledge.[124]

Sri Aurobindo

Spirituality and mind

Spirituality is in its essence an awakening to the inner reality of our being, to a spirit, self, soul which is other than our mind, life and body, an inner aspiration to know, to feel, to be that, to enter into contact with the greater Reality beyond and pervading the universe which inhabits also our own being, to be in communion with It and union with it, and a turning, a conversion, a transformation of our whole being as a result of the aspiration, the contact, the union, a growth or waking into a new becoming or new being, a new self, a new nature.[125]

Sri Aurobindo

Spirituality helps mind but cannot bring about transformation

The mental intelligence and its mental power of reason cannot change the principle and persistent character of human life; it can only affect various mechanisations, manipulations, development and formulations. But neither is mind as a whole, even spiritualised, able to change it; spirituality liberates and illumines the inner being, it helps mind to communicate with what is higher than itself, to escape even from itself; it can purify and uplift by the inner influence the outward nature of individual human beings: but so long as it has to work in the human mass through mind as the instrument, it can exercise an influence on the earth-life but not bring about a transformation of that life. For this reason there has been a prevalent tendency in the spiritual mind to be satisfied with such an influence and in the main to seek fulfilment in other-life elsewhere or to abandon altogether any outward-going endeavour and concentrate solely on an individual spiritual salvation or perfection. A higher instrumental dynamis than mind is needed to transform totally a nature created by the Ignorance.

Sri Aurobindo
The Life Divine, pp. 885-86

The Spiritual Mind

When the spiritual force is able to act, when it begins to have an influence, it jolts the mind's self-satisfaction and, by continuous pressure, begins to make it feel that beyond it there is something higher and truer; then a little of its characteristic vanity gives way under this influence and as soon as it realises that it is limited, ignorant, incapable of reaching the true truth, liberation begins with the possibility of opening to something beyond. But it must *feel* the power, the beauty, the force of this beyond to be able to surrender. It must be able to perceive its incapacity and its limitations in the presence of something higher than itself, otherwise how could it ever feel its own weakness!

Sometimes one single contact is enough, something that makes a little rent in that self-satisfaction; then the yearning to go beyond, the need for a purer light awaken, and with this awakening comes the aspiration to win them, and with this aspiration liberation begins, and one day, breaking all limits, one blossoms in the infinite Light.

If there were not this constant Pressure, simultaneously from within and without, from above and from the profoundest depths, nothing would ever change.

Even with that, how much time is required for things to change! What obstinate resistance in this lower nature, what blind and stupid attachment to the animal ways of the being, what a refusal to liberate oneself!

(Silence)

In the whole manifestation there is an infinite Grace constantly at work to bring the world out of the misery, the obscurity and the stupidity in which it lies. From all time this Grace has been at work, unremitting in its effort, and how many thousands of years were necessary for this world to awaken to the need for something greater, more true, more beautiful.

Everyone can gauge, from the resistance he meets in his own being, the tremendous resistance which the world opposes to the work of the Grace.

And it is only when one understands that *all* external things, all mental constructions, all material efforts are vain, futile, if they are not entirely consecrated to the Light and Force from above, to this Truth which is trying to express itself, that one is ready to make decisive progress. So the only truly effective attitude is a perfect, total, fervent giving of our being to That which is above us and which alone has the power to change everything.

When you open to the Spirit within you it brings you a first foretaste of that higher life which alone is worth living, then comes the will to rise to that, the hope of reaching it, the certitude that this is possible, and finally the strength to make the necessary effort and the resolution to go to the very end.

First one must wake up, then one can conquer.[126]

The Mother

The spiritual being can develop in mind the higher states of being

The nature may obey the psychic entity's intimations, move in an inner light, follow an inner guidance. This is already a considerable evolution and amounts to a beginning at least of a psychic and spiritual transformation. But it is possible to go farther; for the spiritual being, once inwardly liberated, can develop in mind the higher states of being that are its own natural atmosphere and bring down a supramental energy and action which are proper to the Truth-Consciousness; the ordinary mental instrumentation, life-instrumentation, physical instrumentation even, could then be entirely transformed and become parts no longer of an ignorance however much illumined, but of a supramental creation which would be the true action of a spiritual Truth-Consciousness and Knowledge.

At first this truth of the spirit and of spirituality is not self-evident to the mind; man becomes mentally aware of his soul as something other than his body, superior to his normal mind and life, but he has no clear sense of it, only a feeling of some of its effects on his nature. As these effects take a mental form or a life-form, the difference is not firmly and trenchantly drawn, the soul-perception does not acquire a distinct and assured independence. Very commonly indeed, a complex of half-effects of the psychic pressure on the mental and vital parts, a formation mixed with mental aspiration and vital desires, is mistaken for the soul, just as the separative ego is taken for the self, although the self in its true being is universal as well as individual in its essence, – or just as a mixture of mental aspiration and vital enthusiasm and ardour uplifted by some kind of strong or high belief or self-dedication or altruistic eagerness is mistaken for spirituality.[127]

Sri Aurobindo

The first approach of mind to spirit

Up till now what Nature had achieved was an enlarging of the bounds of our surface Knowledge-Ignorance; what it attempted in the spiritual endeavour is to abolish the Ignorance, to go inwards and discover the soul and to become united in consciousness with God and with all existence. This is *the final aim of the mental stage** of evolutionary Nature in man; it is the initial step towards a radical transmutation of the Ignorance into the Knowledge. The spiritual change begins by an influence of the inner being and the higher spiritual mind, an action felt and accepted on the surface; but this by itself can lead only to an illumined mental idealism or to the growth of a religious mind, a religious temperament and some devotion in the heart and piety in the conduct; it is a first approach of mind to spirit, but it cannot make a radical change: more has to be done, we have to live deeper within, we have to exceed our present consciousness and surpass our present status of Nature.[128]

Sri Aurobindo

Spirit, Matter and Mind

And we begin to perceive a complete aim for our synthesis of Yoga.

Spirit is the crown of universal existence; Matter is its basis; Mind is the link between the two. Spirit is that which is eternal; Mind and Matter are its workings. Spirit is that which is concealed and has to be revealed; mind and body are the means by which it seeks to reveal itself. Spirit is the image of the Lord of the Yoga; mind and body are the means He has provided for reproducing that image in phenomenal existence. All Nature is an attempt at a progressive revelation of the concealed Truth, a more and more successful reproduction of the divine image.[129]

Sri Aurobindo

*

* Emphasis ours. (Ed.)

The Spiritual Mind

In Mind the knowledge of the unity of all aspects is lost on the surface, the consciousness is plunged into engrossing, exclusive separate affirmations; but there too, even in the Mind's ignorance, the total reality still remains behind the exclusive absorption and can be recovered in the form of a profound mental intuition or else in the idea or sentiment of an underlying truth of integral oneness; in the spiritual mind this can develop into an ever-present experience.[130]

Sri Aurobindo

Mind as a derivation from the fullness of self

The mind, when we trace the descent of the self towards matter, we see as a derivation which travels away from the fullness of self, the fullness of its light and being and which lives in a division and diversion, not in the body of the sun, but first in its nearer and then in its far-off rays. There is a highest intuitive mind which receives more nearly the supramental truth, but even this is a formation which conceals the direct and greater real knowledge. There is an intellectual mind which is a luminous half-opaque lid which intercepts and reflects in a radiantly distorting and suppressively modifying atmosphere the truth known to the supermind. There is a still lower mind built on the foundation of the senses between which and the sun of knowledge there is a thick cloud, an emotional and a sensational mist and vapour with here and there lightnings and illuminations. There is a vital mind which is shut away even from the light of intellectual truth, and lower still in submental life and matter the spirit involves itself entirely as if in a sleep and a night, a sleep plunged in a dim and yet poignant nervous dream, the night of a mechanical somnambulist energy. It is a re-evolution of the spirit out of this lowest state in which we find ourselves at a height above the lower creation having taken it up all in us and reaching so far in our ascent only the light of the well-developed mental reason. The full powers of self-knowledge and the illumined will of the spirit are still beyond us above the mind and reason in supramental Nature.[131]

Sri Aurobindo

The achievement of the spiritual mind in man

Yet, although the psychic transformation is one necessary condition of the total transformation of our existence, it is not all that is needed for the largest spiritual change. In the first place, since this is the individual soul in Nature, it can open to the hidden diviner ranges of our being and receive and reflect their light and power and experience, but another, a spiritual transformation from above is needed for us to possess our self in its universality and transcendence. By itself the psychic being at a certain stage might be content to create a formation of truth, good and beauty and make that its station; at a farther stage it might become passively subject to the world-self, a mirror of the universal existence, consciousness, power, delight, but not their full participant or possessor. Although more nearly and thrillingly united to the cosmic consciousness in knowledge, emotion and even appreciation through the senses, it might become purely recipient and passive, remote from mastery and action in the world; or, one with the static self behind the cosmos, but separate inwardly from the world-movement, losing its individuality in its Source, it might return to that Source and have neither the will nor the power any further for that which was its ultimate mission here, to lead the nature also towards its divine realisation. For the psychic being came into Nature from the Self, the Divine, and it can turn back from nature to the silent Divine through the silence of the self and a supreme spiritual immobility. Again, an eternal portion of the Divine*, this part is by the law of the Infinite inseparable from its Divine Whole, this part is indeed itself that Whole, except in its frontal appearance, its frontal separative self-experience; it may awaken to that reality and plunge into it to the apparent extinction or at least the merging of the individual existence. A small nucleus here in the mass of our ignorant Nature, so that it is described in the Upanishad as no bigger than a man's thumb, it can by the spiritual influx enlarge itself and embrace the whole world with the heart and mind in an intimate communion or oneness. Or it may become aware of its eternal companion and elect to live for ever in His presence, in an imperishable union and oneness as the eternal lover with the eternal Beloved, which of all spiritual experiences is the most intense in beauty and rapture. All these are great and splendid achievements of our spiritual self-finding, but they are not necessarily the last end and entire consummation; more is possible.

For these are achievements of the spiritual mind in man**; they are *movements of that mind*** passing beyond itself, but *on its own plane***, into the splendours of the Spirit.[132]

Sri Aurobido

---

* Gita, XV, 7.
** Emphasis ours. (Ed.)

The lines of achievement of the spiritual mind

Mind, even at its highest stages far beyond our present mentality, acts yet in its nature by division; it takes the aspects of the Eternal and treats each aspect as if it were the whole truth of the Eternal being and can find in each its own perfect fulfilment. Even it erects them into opposites and creates a whole range of these opposites, the Silence of the Divine and the divine Dynamis, the immobile Brahman aloof from existence, without qualities, and the active Brahman with qualities, Lord of existence, Being and Becoming, the Divine Person and an impersonal pure Existence; it can then cut itself away from the one and plunge itself into the other as the sole abiding truth of existence. It can regard the Person as the sole Reality or the Impersonal as alone true; it can regard the Lover as only a means of expression of eternal Love or love as only the self-expression of the Lover; it can see beings as only personal powers of an impersonal Existence or impersonal existence as only a state of the one being, the infinite Person. Its spiritual achievement, its road of passage towards the supreme aim will follow these dividing lines. But beyond this movement of spiritual Mind is the higher experience of the Supermind Truth-Consciousness; there these opposites disappear and these partialities are relinquished in the rich totality of a supreme and integral realisation of eternal Being.[133]

Sri Aurobindo

The spiritual man's mind

For the spiritual man the mind's dream of perfect beauty is realised in an eternal love, beauty and delight that has no dependence and is equal behind all objective appearances; its dream of perfect Truth in the supreme, self-existent, self-apparent and eternal Verity which never varies, but explains and is the secret of all variations and the goal of all progress; its dream of perfect action in the omnipotent and self-guiding Law that is inherent for ever in all things and translates itself here in the rhythm of the worlds. What is fugitive vision or constant effort of creation in the brilliant Self is an eternally existing Reality in the Self that knows* and is the Lord.[134]

Sri Aurobindo

The tendency of the spiritualised mind is to go upwards

The tendency of the spiritualised mind is to go on upwards and, since above itself the mind loses its hold on forms, it is into a vast formless and featureless impersonality that it enters. It becomes aware of the unchanging Self, the sheer Spirit, the pure bareness of an essential Existence, the formless Infinite and the nameless Absolute. This culmination can be arrived at more directly by tending immediately beyond all forms and figures, beyond all ideas of good or evil or true or false or beautiful or unbeautiful to That which exceeds all dualities, to the experience of a supreme oneness, infinity, eternity or other ineffable sublimation of the mind's ultimate and extreme percept of Self or Spirit. A spiritualised consciousness is achieved and the life falls quiet, the body ceases

---

* The Unified, in whom thought is concentrated, who is all delight and enjoyer of delight, the wise.... He is the Lord of all, the Omniscient, the inner Guide. – *Mandukya Upanishad*, 5, 6.

to need and to clamour, the soul itself merges into the spiritual silence. But this transformation through the mind does not give us the integral transformation; the psychic transmutation is replaced by a spiritual change on the rare and high summits, but this is not the complete divine dynamisation of Nature.[135]

Sri Aurobindo

The ascension of Mind

But once this entry into the inner being is accomplished, the inner Self is found to be capable of an opening, an ascent upwards into things beyond our present mental level; that is the second spiritual possibility in us. The first most ordinary result is a discovery of a vast static and silent Self which we feel to be our real or our basic existence, the foundation of all else that we are... In the dynamic movement, the resultant greater action of Consciousness-Force may present itself either simply as a pure spiritual dynamis not otherwise determinate in its character or it may reveal a spiritual mind-range where mind is no longer ignorant of the Reality, – not yet a supermind level, but deriving from the supramental Truth-Consciousness and still luminous with something of its knowledge.

It is in the latter alternative that we find the secret we are seeking, the means of the transition, the needed step towards a supramental transformation; for we perceive a graduality of ascent, a communication with a more and more deep and immense light and power from above, a scale of intensities which can be regarded as so many stairs in the ascension of Mind or in a descent into Mind from That which is beyond it. We are aware of a sealike downpour of masses of a spontaneous knowledge which assumes the nature of Thought but

The Spiritual Mind

has a different character from the process of thought to which we are accustomed; for there is nothing here of seeking, no trace of mental construction, no labour of speculation or difficult discovery; it is an automatic and spontaneous knowledge from a Higher Mind that seems to be in possession of Truth and not in search of hidden and withheld realities. One observes that this Thought is much more capable than the mind of including at once a mass of knowledge in a single view; it has a cosmic character, not the stamp of an individual thinking.[136]

Sri Aurobindo

Beyond the spiritual mind

A sudden turn can come, a road appear.
A greater Mind may see a greater Truth,
Or we may find when all the rest has failed
Hid in ourselves the key of perfect change.
Ascending from the soil where creep our days,
Earth's consciousness may marry with the Sun,
Our mortal life ride on the spirit's wings,
Our finite thoughts commune with the Infinite.

   In the bright kingdoms of the rising Sun
All is a birth into a power of light:
All here deformed guards there its happy shape,
Here all is mixed and marred, there pure and whole;
Yet each is a passing step, a moment's phase.
Awake to a greater Truth beyond her acts,
The mediatrix sat and saw her works
And felt the marvel in them and the force
But knew the power behind the face of Time:
She did the task, obeyed the knowledge given,
Her deep heart yearned towards great ideal things
And from the light looked out to wider light:
A brilliant hedge drawn round her narrowed her power;
Faithful to her limited sphere she toiled, but knew
Its highest, widest seeing was a half-search,
Its mightiest acts a passage or a stage.
For not by Reason was creation made
And not by Reason can the Truth be seen
Which through the veils of thought, the screens of sense
Hardly the spirit's vision can descry
Dimmed by the imperfection of its means:...
For nothing is known while aught remains concealed;
The Truth is known only when all is seen.[137]

                                           Sri Aurobindo

From the spiritualised mind to the Supermind

There is an ascension still to be made from this height, by which the spiritualised mind will exceed itself and transmute into a supramental power of knowledge. Already in the process of spiritualisation it will have begun to pass out of the brilliant poverty of the human intellect; it will mount successively into the pure broad reaches of a higher mind, and next into the gleaming belts of a still greater free Intelligence illumined with a Light from above. At this point it will begin to feel more freely, admit with a less mixed response the radiant beginnings of an Intuition, not illumined, but luminous in itself, true in itself, no longer entirely mental and therefore subjected to the abundant intrusion of error. Here too is not an end, for it must rise beyond into the very domain of that untruncated Intuition, the first direct light from the self-awareness of essential Being and, beyond it, attain that from which this light comes. For there is an Overmind behind Mind, a Power more original and dynamic which supports Mind, sees it as a diminished radiation from itself, uses it as a transmitting belt of passage downward or an instrument for the creations of the Ignorance. The last step of the ascension would be the surpassing of Overmind itself or its return into its own still greater origin, its conversion into the supramental light of the Divine Gnosis. For there in the supramental Light is the seat of the divine Truth-consciousness that has native in it, as no other consciousness below it can have, the power to organise the works of a Truth which is no longer tarnished by the shadow of the cosmic Inconscience and Ignorance. There to reach and thence to bring down a supramental dynamism that can transform the Ignorance is the distant but imperative supreme goal of the integral Yoga.[138]

Sri Aurobindo

GRADATIONS OF MANIFESTATION

THE SUPREME

Sachchidananda — Unmanifest, making possible every kind of manifestation

SACHCHIDANANDA IN MANIFESTATION

The Supreme Planes of Infinite Consciousness
1) Sat (implying Chit-Tapas and Ananda
2) Chit (implying Sat and Ananda)
3) Ananda (implying Sat and Chit-Tapas)

SUPERMIND OR DIVINE GNOSIS

(The Self-Determining Infinite Consciousness)
From the point of view of our ascent upwards this is the Truth-Consciousness as distinguished from all below that belongs to the separative Ignorance.

OVERMIND OR MAYA

Overmind takes all Truth that comes down to it from the Supermind, but sets up each Truth as a separate force and idea capable of conflicting with the others as well as cooperating with them. Each overmental being has his own world, each force has its own play and throws itself out to realise its own fulfilment in the cosmic play. All is possible; and from this separative seat of conflicting and even mutually negating possibilities comes too, as soon as mind, life and matter are thrown out into play the possibility of ignorance, unconsciousness, falsehood, death and suffering.[139]

Sri Aurobindo

OVERMIND GRADATION TO MIND
OVERMIND GNOSIS

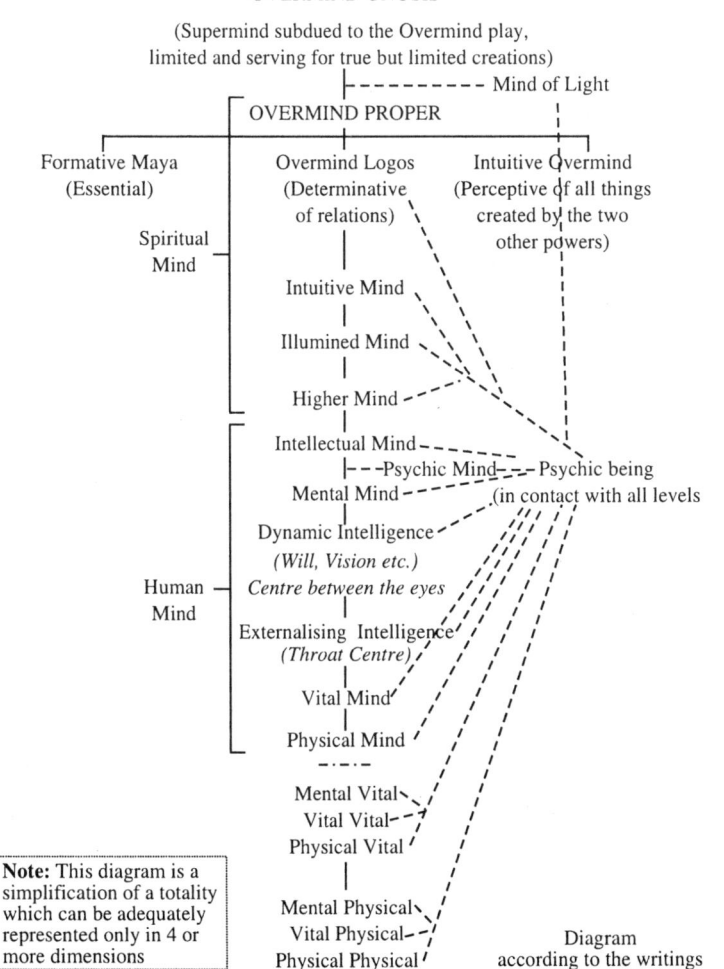

(Supermind subdued to the Overmind play,
limited and serving for true but limited creations)

------- Mind of Light

OVERMIND PROPER

Formative Maya (Essential)

Overmind Logos (Determinative of relations)

Intuitive Overmind (Perceptive of all things created by the two other powers)

Spiritual Mind

- Intuitive Mind
- Illumined Mind
- Higher Mind

Human Mind

- Intellectual Mind
- Psychic Mind --- Psychic being
- Mental Mind (in contact with all levels)
- Dynamic Intelligence *(Will, Vision etc.)*
- *Centre between the eyes*
- Externalising Intelligence *(Throat Centre)*
- Vital Mind
- Physical Mind

- Mental Vital
- Vital Vital
- Physical Vital

- Mental Physical
- Vital Physical
- Physical Physical

Note: This diagram is a simplification of a totality which can be adequately represented only in 4 or more dimensions

Diagram according to the writings of Sri Aurobindo

TOWARDS SUPERMIND

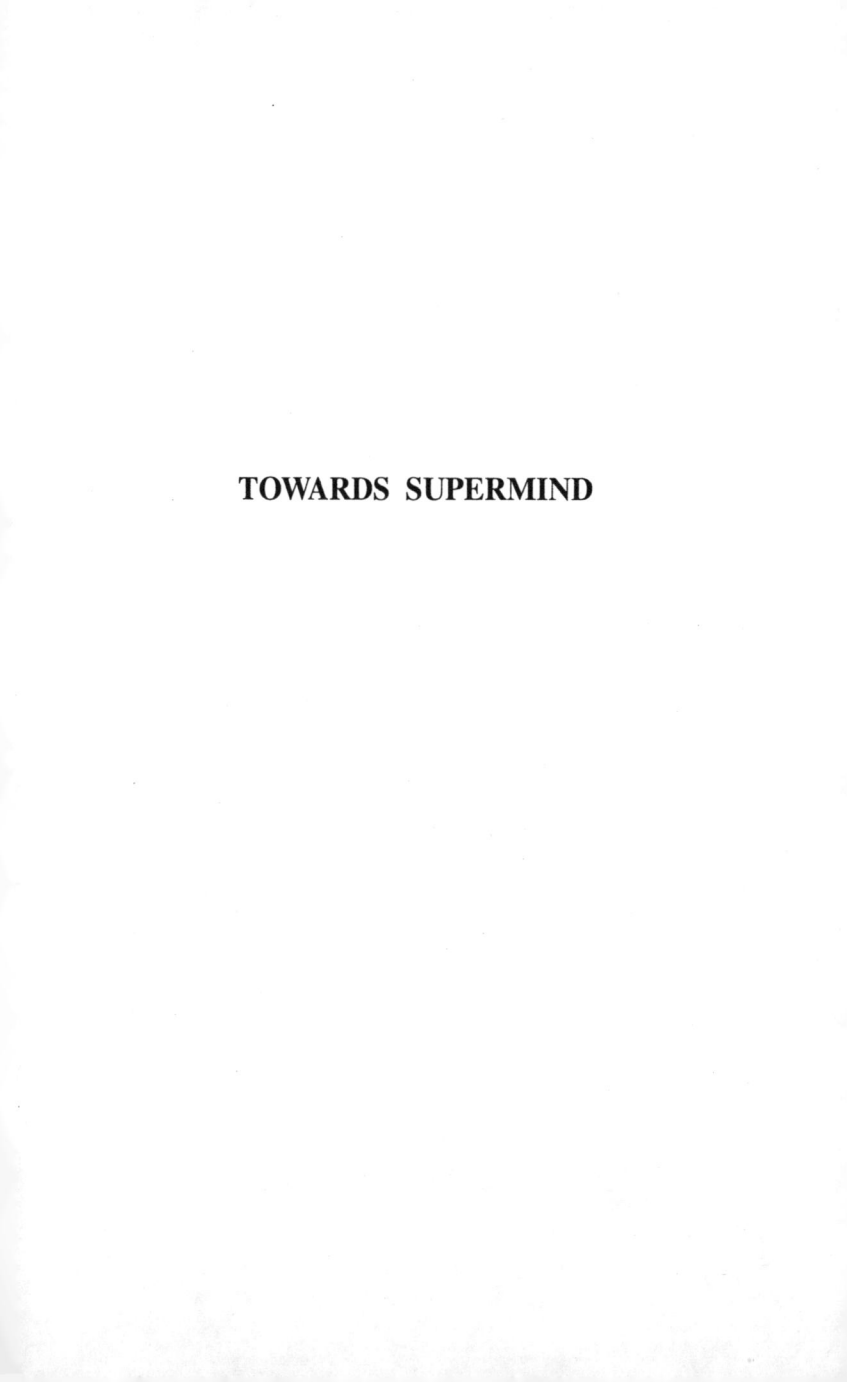

The Kingdom Within

There is a kingdom of the spirit's ease
    It is not in this helpless swirl of thought,
    Foam from the world-sea or spray-whisper caught,
With which we build mind's shifting symmetries,
Nor in life's stuff of passionate unease,
    Nor the heart's unsure emotions frailty wrought
    Nor trivial clipped sense-joys soon led* to nought
Nor in this body's solid transiences.

Wider behind than the vast universe
    Our spirit scans the drama and the stir,
    A peace, a light, an ecstasy, a power
Waiting at the end of blindness and the curse
    That veils it from its ignorant minister,
    The grandeur of its free eternal hour.[140]

                                         Sri Aurobindo

* brought

TOWARDS SUPERMIND

Man's rise to the Infinite

The instrument of man is mind and thinking and willing mind-force – just as the instrument of the animal is life instinct and feeling and remembering life-force and the instrument of the plant and tree existence is the vital push and the dynamism of material energy turning into force of life. As these lower states developed up to a point at which Mind-intelligence could descend into the organised living body and take up the earth-past to mentalise and transform it, so Mind in man has to develop up to a point at which a consciousness greater than Mind can descend into the mind and living body and take up the human material to supramentalise and transform it into godhead. This is man's rise to the Infinite.

... a consciousness greater than mind has already been felt by many of those who have climbed to the human summits and to the glow that has come from above they have given many names, *bodhi*, intuition, gnosis. But these things are only the faint edge of that greater light thrust into the pallid twilight that we call mind. Only when the lid between mind and supermind has been utterly rent apart and the full power of the sun of a divine Gnosis can pour down – not breaking through mind as in diminished and deflected beams – and transform the whole mind and life and body of the human creature, can man's labour finish. Then only shall begin the divine play and the free out-pouring of the liberated self-creating Spirit.

To rise into this greater consciousness above our mental level of humanity as man has risen above the level of the life-mind of the beast, to grow from mind into supermind, from twilight into light, from the mind's half-consciousness into what is now to us superconscient, from a narrow imprisoned ego into the transcendent and universalised individual, from a struggling half-effective into a throned and master power, from little transient joys and sorrows into an unalloyed divine delight, this is the goal of our journey, the secret of our struggle.

This is our way of emergence from the now dark riddle of the earth and unsolved problem of human life. If there were not this secret sense in all we are and do, there would be no significance in the material world and no justification for our earth-existence.

A gnostic superman is the future master of the earth and rescuer of the divine meaning of the ambiguous terms of this great world-enigma.[141]

Sri Aurobindo

Human mind reaches beyond itself

There are several directions in which human mind reaches beyond itself, tends towards self-exceeding; these are precisely the necessary lines of contact or veiled or half-veiled passages which connect it with higher grades of consciousness of the self-manifesting Spirit. First, we have noted the place Intuition occupies in the human means of knowledge, and Intuition is in its very nature a projection of the characteristic action of these higher grades into the mind of Ignorance. It is true that in human mind its action is largely hidden by the interventions of our normal intelligence; a pure intuition is a rare occurrence in our mental activity: for what we call by the name is usually a point of direct knowledge which is immediately caught and coated over with mental stuff, so that it serves only as an invisible or a very tiny nucleus of a crystallisation which is in its mass intellectual or otherwise mental in character; or else the flash of intuition is quickly replaced or intercepted, before it has a chance of manifesting itself, by a rapid imitative mental movement, insight or quick perception or some swift-leaping process of thought which owes its appearance to the stimulus of the coming intuition but obstructs its entry or covers it with a substituted mental suggestion true or erroneous but in either case not the authentic intuitive movement. Nevertheless, the fact of this intervention from above, the fact that behind all our original thinking or authentic perception of things there is a veiled, a half-veiled or a swift unveiled intuitive element is enough to establish a connection between mind and what is above it; it opens a passage of communication and of entry into the superior spirit-ranges.... *Impersonality** is the first character of cosmic self; *universality***, non-limitation by the single or limiting point of view, is the character of cosmic perception and knowledge: this tendency is therefore a widening, however rudimentary, of these restricted mind areas towards cosmicity, towards a quality which is the very character of the higher mental planes, – towards that superconscient cosmic Mind which, we have suggested, must in the nature of things be the original mind-action of which ours is only a derivative and inferior process. Again, there is not an entire absence of penetration from above into our mental limits. The phenomena of genius are really the result of such a penetration, – veiled, no doubt, because the light of the superior consciousness not only acts within narrow limits, usually in

---

* Emphasis ours. (Ed.)
** Emphasis ours. (Ed.)

a special field, without any regulated separate organisation of its characteristic energies, often indeed quite fitfully, erratically and with a supernormal or abnormal irresponsible governance, but also in entering the mind it subdues and adapts itself to mind substance so that it is only a modified or diminished dynamis that reaches us, not all the original divine luminosity of what might be called the overhead consciousness beyond us. Still the phenomena of *inspiration**, of revelatory vision or of intuitive perception and intuitive discernment, surpassing our less illumined or less powerful normal mind-action, are there and their origin is unmistakable. Finally, there is the vast and multitudinous field of *mystic and spiritual experience*,* and here the gates already lie wide open to the possibility of extending our consciousness beyond its present limits, – unless, indeed, by an obscurantism that refuses to inquire or an attachment to our boundaries of mental normality we shut them or turn away from the vistas they open before us. But in our present investigation we cannot afford to neglect the possibilities which these domains of mankind's endeavour bring near to us, or the added knowledge of oneself and of the veiled Reality which is their gift to human mind, the greater light which arms them with the right to act upon us and is the innate power of their existence.[142]

Sri Aurobindo

Spirit, Atman and Jivatman

The Spirit is the Atman, Brahman, Essential Divine.[143]

*

* Emphasis ours. (Ed.)

The Jivatman or spirit, as it is usually called in English, is self-existent above the manifested or instrumental being – it is superior to birth and death, always the same, the individual Self or Atman. It is the eternal true being of the individual.[144]

*

The psychic being realises its oneness with the true being, the Jivatman, but it does not change into it.[145]

Sri Aurobindo

*

The Atman is the Self or Spirit that remains above, pure and stainless, unaffected by the stains of life, by desire and ego and ignorance. It is realised as the true being of the individual, but also more widely as the *same* being in all and as the Self in the cosmos; it has also a self-existence above the individual and cosmos and it is then called the Paramatma, the supreme Divine Being.[146]

Sri Aurobindo

Atman, our true self, is Brahman; it is pure indivisible Being, self-luminous, self-concentrated in consciousness, self-concentrated in force, self-delighted. Its existence is light and bliss. It is timeless, spaceless and free.[147]

Sri Aurobindo

*

The Self or Atman being free and superior to birth and

death, the experience of the Jivatman and its unity with the supreme or universal Self brings the sense of liberation, it is this which is necessary for the supreme spiritual deliverance: but for the transformation of the life and nature the awakening of the psychic being and its rule over the nature are indispensable.[148]

Sri Aurobindo

*

The Jivatman, spark-soul and psychic being are three different forms of the same reality and they must not be mixed up together, as that confuses the clearness of the inner experience.[149]

Sri Aurobindo

*

The Jiva is realised as the individual Self, Atman, the central being above the Nature, calm, untouched by the movements of Nature, but supporting their evolution though not involved in it. Through this realisation silence, freedom, wideness, mastery, purity, sense of universality in the individual as one centre of this divine universality become the normal experience. The psychic is realised as the Purusha behind the heart. It is not universalised like the Jivatman, but is the individual soul supporting from its place behind the heart-centre the mental, vital, physical, psychic evolution of the being in Nature. Its realisation brings bhakti, self-giving, surrender, turning of all the movements Godward, discrimination and choice of all that belongs to the Divine Truth, Good, Beauty, rejection of all that is false, evil, ugly, discordant, union through love and sympathy with all existence, openness to the Truth of the Self and the Divine.[150]

Sri Aurobindo

*

As for the psychic being, it enters into the evolution, enters into the body at birth and goes out of it at death; but the Jivatman, as I know it, is unborn and eternal although upholding the manifested personality from above.[151]

Sri Aurobindo

The widening into the inner mind

There are two successive movements of consciousness, difficult but well within our capacity, by which we can have access to the superior gradations of our conscious existence. There is first a movement inward by which, instead of living in our surface mind, we break the wall between our external and our now subliminal self; this can be brought about by a gradual effort and discipline or by a vehement transition, sometimes a forceful involuntary rupture, – the latter by no means safe for the limited human mind accustomed to live securely only within its normal limits, – but in either way, safe or unsafe, the thing can be done. What we discover within this secret part of ourselves is an inner being, a soul, an inner mind, an inner life, an inner subtle-physical entity which is much larger in its potentialities, more plastic, more powerful, more capable of a manifold knowledge and dynamism than our surface mind, life or body; especially, it is capable of a direct communication with the universal forces, movements, objects of the cosmos, a direct feeling and opening to them, a direct action on them and even a widening of itself beyond the limits of the personal mind, the personal life, the body, so that it feels itself more and more a universal being no longer limited by the existing walls of our too narrow mental, vital, physical existence. This widening can extend itself to a complete entry into the consciousness of cosmic Mind, into unity with the universal Life, even into a oneness with universal Matter.[152]

Sri Aurobindo

The inner mind

The inner mind is something very wide projecting itself into the infinite and finally identifying itself with the infinity of universal Mind. When we break out of the narrow limits of the external physical mind we begin to see inwardly and to feel this wideness, in the end this universality and infinity of the mental self-space.[153]

Sri Aurobindo

Inner mind and poetic vision

But there are other influences which can suffuse and modify the pure poetic intelligence, making it perhaps less clear by limitation but more vivid, colourful, vivid with various lights and hues; it becomes less intellectual, more made of vision and a flame of insight. Very often this comes by an infiltration of the veiled inner Mind which is within us and has its own wider and deeper fields and subtler movements, – and can bring also the tinge of a higher afflatus to the poetic intelligence, sometimes a direct uplifting towards what is beyond it.

There is also a plane of dynamic Vision which is a part of the inner Mind and perhaps should be called not a plane but a province. There are many kinds of vision in the inner Mind and not this dynamic vision alone.[154]

Sri Aurobindo

The higher mind

Our first decisive step out of our human intelligence, our normal mentality, is an ascent into a higher Mind, a mind no longer of mingled light and obscurity or half-light, but a *large clarity of the Spirit**. Its basic substance is a unitarian sense of being with a powerful multiple dynamisation capable of the formation of a multitude of aspects of knowledge, ways of action, forms and significances of becoming, of all of which there is a spontaneous inherent knowledge. It is therefore a power that has proceeded from the Overmind, – but with the Supermind as its ulterior origin, – as all these greater powers have proceeded: but its special character, its activity of consciousness are dominated by Thought; it is a luminous thought-mind, a mind of Spirit-born conceptual knowledge. An all-awareness emerging from the original identity, carrying the truths the identity held in itself, conceiving swiftly, victoriously, multitudinously, formulating and by self-power of the Idea effectually realising its conceptions, is the character of this greater mind of knowledge. This kind of cognition is the last that emerges from the original spiritual identity before the initiation of a separative knowledge, base of the Ignorance; it is therefore the first that meets us when we rise from conceptive and ratiocinative mind, our best-organised

---

* Emphasis ours. (Ed.)

knowledge-power of the Ignorance, into the realms of the Spirit; it is, indeed, the spiritual parent of our conceptive mental ideation, and it is natural that this leading power of our mentality should, when it goes beyond itself, pass into its immediate source.[155]

Sri Aurobindo

The higher mind is more powerful than reason

The higher mind in man is something other, loftier, purer, vaster, more powerful than the reason or logical intelligence. The animal is a vital and sensational being; man, it is said, is distinguished from the animal by the possession of reason. But that is a very summary, a very imperfect and misleading account of the matter. For reason is only a particular and limited utilitarian and instrumental activity that proceeds from something much greater than itself, from a power that dwells in an ether more luminous, wider, illimitable. The true and ultimate, as distinguished from the immediate or intermediate importance of our observing, reasoning, inquiring, judging intelligence is that it prepares the human being for the right reception and right action of a Light from above which must progressively replace in him the obscure light from below that guides the animal. The latter also has a rudimentary reason, a kind of thought, a soul, a will and keen emotions; even though less developed, its psychology is yet the same in kind as man's. But all these capacities in the animal are automatically moved and strictly limited, almost even constituted by the lower nervous being. All animal perceptions, sensibilities, activities are ruled by nervous and vital instincts, cravings, needs, satisfactions, of which the nexus is the life-impulse and vital desire. Man too is bound, but less bound, to this automatism of the vital nature. Man can bring an enlightened will, an enlightened thought and enlightened emotions to the difficult work of his self-development; he can more and more subject to these more conscious and reflecting guides the inferior function of desire. In proportion as he can thus master and enlighten his lower self, he is man and no longer an animal. When he can begin to replace desire altogether by a still greater enlightened thought and sight and will in touch with the Infinite, consciously subject to a diviner will than his own, linked to a more universal and transcendent knowledge, he has commenced the ascent towards the superman; he is on his upward march towards the Divine.[156]

Sri Aurobindo

Aspects of the higher mind: cognition and will

It [higher consciousness] can freely express itself in single ideas, but its most characteristic movement is a mass ideation, a system or totality of truth-seeing at a single view; the relations of idea with idea, of truth with truth are not established by logic but pre-exist and emerge already self-seen in the integral whole. There is an initiation into forms of an ever-present but till now inactive knowledge, not a system of conclusions from premises or data; this thought is a self-revelation of eternal Wisdom, not an acquired knowledge. Large aspects of truth come into view in which the ascending Mind, if it chooses, can dwell with satisfaction and, after its former manner, live in them as in a structure; but if progress is to be made, these structures can constantly expand into a larger structure or several of them combine themselves into a provisional greater whole on the way to a yet unachieved integrality. In the end there is a great totality of truth known and experienced but still a totality capable of infinite enlargement because there is no end to the aspects of knowledge, *nāstyanto vistarasya me.*

This is the Higher Mind in its aspect of cognition; but there is also the aspect of will, of dynamic effectuation of the Truth: here we find that this greater more brilliant Mind works always on the rest of the being, the mental will, the heart and its feelings, the life, the body, through the power of thought, through the idea-force. It seeks to purify through knowledge, to deliver through knowledge, to create by the innate power of knowledge. The idea is put into the heart or the life as a force to be accepted and worked out; the heart and life become conscious of the idea and respond to its dynamisms and their substance begins to modify itself in that sense, so that the feelings and actions become the vibrations of this higher wisdom, are informed with it, filled with the emotion and the sense of it: the will and the life impulses are similarly charged with its power and its urge of self-effectuation; even in the body the idea works so that, for example, the potent thought and will of health replaces its faith in illness and its consent to illness, or the idea* of strength calls in the substance, power, motion, vibration of strength; the idea generates the force and form proper to the idea and imposes it on our substance of Mind, Life or Matter. It is in this way that the first working proceeds; it charges the whole being with a new and superior consciousness, lays the foundations of change, prepares it for a superior truth of existence.[157]

Sri Aurobindo

---

* The word expressing the idea has the same power if it is surcharged with the spiritual force; that is the rationale of the Indian use of the *mantra*.

The formation of a luminous mind

The transition from mind to supermind is not only the substitution of a greater instrument of thought and knowledge, but a change and conversion of the whole consciousness.... The next step is the formation of a luminous mind of intuitive experience, thought, will, feeling, sense from which the intermixture of the lesser mind and the imitative intuition are progressively eliminated: this is a process of purification, *śuddhi*, necessary to the new formation and perfection, *siddhi*. At the same time there is the disclosure above the mind of the source of the intuitive action and a more and more organised functioning of a true supramental consciousness acting not in the mind but on its own higher plane. This draws up into itself in the end the intuitive mentality it has created as its representative and assumes the charge of the whole activity of the consciousness. The process is progressive and for a long time chequered by admixture and the necessity of a return upon the lower movements in order to correct and transform them. The higher and the lower power act sometimes alternately, – the consciousness, descending back from the heights it had attained to its former level but always with some change, – but sometimes together and with a sort of mutual reference. The mind eventually becomes wholly intuitivised and exists only as a passive channel for the supramental action; but this condition too is not ideal and presents, besides, still a certain obstacle, because the higher action has still to pass through a retarding and diminishing conscious substance, – that of the physical consciousness. The final stage of the change will come when the supermind occupies and supramentalises the whole being and turns even the vital and physical sheaths into moulds of itself, responsive, subtle and instinct with its powers. Man then becomes wholly the superman. This is at least the natural and integral process.[158]

The Illumined Mind

This greater Force is that of the Illumined Mind, a Mind no longer of higher Thought, but of spiritual light. Here the clarity of the spiritual intelligence, its tranquil daylight, gives place or subordinates itself to an intense lustre, a splendour and illumination of the Spirit: a play of lightnings of spiritual truth and power breaks from above into the consciousness and adds to the calm and wide enlightenment and the vast descent of peace which characterise or accompany the action of the larger conceptual-spiritual principle, a fiery ardour of realisation and a rapturous ecstasy of knowledge. A downpour of inwardly visible Light very usually envelops this action; for it must be noted that, contrary to our ordinary conceptions, light is not primarily a material creation and the sense or vision of light accompanying the inner illumination is not merely a subjective visual image or a symbolic phenomenon: light is primarily a spiritual manifestation of the Divine Reality illuminative and creative; material light is a subsequent representation or conversion of it into matter for the purposes of the material Energy. There is also in this descent the arrival of a greater dynamic, a golden drive, a luminous "enthousiasmos" of inner force and power which replaces the comparatively slow and deliberate process of the Higher Mind by a swift, sometimes a vehement, almost a violent impetus of rapid transformation.

The Illumined Mind does not work primarily by thought, but by vision; thought is here only a subordinate movement expressive of sight. The human mind, which relies mainly on thought, conceives that to be the highest or the main process of knowledge, but in the spiritual order thought is a secondary and a not indispensable process. In its form of verbal thought, it can almost be described as a concession made by Knowledge to the Ignorance, because that Ignorance is incapable of making truth wholly lucid and intelligible to itself in all its extent and manifold implications except through the clarifying precision of significant sound; it cannot do without this device to give to ideas an exact outline and an expressive body. But it is evident that this is a device, a machinery; thought in itself, in its origin on the higher levels of consciousness, is a perception, a cognitive seizing of the object or of some truth of things which is a powerful but still a minor and secondary result of spiritual vision, a comparatively external and superficial regard of the self upon the self, the subject upon itself or something of itself as object; for all there is a diversity and multiplicity of the self. In mind there is a surface response of perception to the contact of an observed or discovered object, fact or truth and a consequent conceptual formulation of it; but in the spiritual light there is a deeper perceptive response from the very substance of consciousness and a comprehending formulation in that substance, an exact figure of revelatory ideograph in the stuff of the being, – nothing more, no verbal representation is needed for the precision and completeness of this thought-knowledge. Thought creates a representative image of Truth; it offers that to the mind as a means of holding Truth and making it an object of knowledge; but the body itself of Truth is caught and exactly held in the sunlight of a deeper spiritual sight to which the representative figure created by thought is secondary and derivative, powerful for communication of knowl-

Towards Supermind

edge, but not indispensable for reception or possession of knowledge.

A consciousness that proceeds by sight, the consciousness of the seer, is a greater power for knowledge than the consciousness of the thinker. The perceptual power of the inner sight is greater and more direct than the perceptual power of thought: it is a spiritual sense that seizes something of the substance of Truth and not only her figure; but it outlines the figure also and at the same time catches the significance of the figure, and it can embody her with a finer and bolder revealing outline and a larger comprehension and power of totality than thought-conception can manage. As the Higher Mind brings a greater consciousness into the being through the spiritual idea and its power of truth, so the Illumined Mind brings in a still greater consciousness through a Truth-sight and Truth-light and its seeing and seizing power. It can effect a more powerful and dynamic integration; it illumines the thought-mind with a direct inner vision and inspiration, brings a spiritual sight into the heart and a spiritual light and energy into its feeling and emotion, imparts to the life-force a spiritual urge, a truth inspiration that dynamises the action and exalts the life-movements; it infuses into the sense a direct and total power of spiritual sensation so that our vital and physical being can contact and meet concretely, quite as intensely as the mind and emotion can conceive and perceive and feel, the Divine in all things; it throws on the physical mind a transforming light that breaks its limitations, its conservative inertia, replaces its narrow thought-power and its doubts by sight and pours luminosity and consciousness into the very cells of the body. In the transformation by the Higher Mind the spiritual sage and thinker would find his total and dynamic fulfilment; in the transformation by the

Illumined Mind there would be a similar fulfilment for the seer, the illumined mystic, those in whom the soul lives in vision and in a direct sense and experience: for it is from these higher sources that they receive their light and to rise into that light and live there would be their ascension to their native empire.[159]

Sri Aurobindo

Poetry of the illumined mind and intuition

The poetry of the illumined mind is usually full of a play of lights and colours, brilliant and striking in phrase, for illumination makes the Truth vivid – it acts usually by a luminous rush. The poetry of the Intuition may have play of colour and bright lights, but it does not depend on them – it may be quite bare; it tells by a sort of close intimacy with the Truth, an inward expression of it. The illumined mind sometimes gets rid of its trappings, but even then it always keeps a sort of lustrousness of robe which is its characteristic.[160]

Sri Aurobindo

Intuitive mind or intuitive reason

There is, indeed, a higher form of the *buddhi* that can be called the intuitive mind or intuitive reason, and this by its intuitions, its inspirations, its swift revelatory vision, its luminous insight and discrimination can do the work of the reason with a higher power, a swifter action, a greater and spontaneous certitude. It acts in a self-light of the truth which does not depend upon the torch-flares of the sense-mind and its limited uncertain percepts; it proceeds not by intelligent but by visional concepts: it is a kind of truth-vision, truth-hearing, truth-memory, direct truth-discernment. This true and authentic intuition must be distinguished from a power of the ordinary mental reason which is too easily confused with it, the power of involved reasoning that reaches its conclusion by a bound and does not need the ordinary steps of the logical mind. The logical reason proceeds pace after pace and tries the sureness of each step like a man who is walking over unsafe ground and has to test by the hesitating touch of his foot each span of soil that he perceives with his eye. But this other supralogical process of the reason is a motion of rapid insight or swift discernment; it proceeds by a stride or leap, like a man who springs from one sure spot to another point of sure footing, – or at least held by him to be sure. He sees the space he covers in one compact and flashing view, but he does not distinguish or measure either by eye or touch its successions, features and circumstances. This movement has something of the sense of power of the intuition, something of its velocity, some appearance of its light and certainty, and we always are apt to take it for the intuition. But our assumption is an error and, if we trust to it, may lead us into grievous blunders.[161]

Sri Aurobindo

The intuitive mentality is still mind and not gnosis

The intuitive mentality is still mind and not gnosis. It is indeed a light from the supermind, but modified and diminished by the stuff of mind in which it works, and stuff of mind means always a basis of ignorance. The intuitive mind is not yet the wide sunlight of truth, but a constant play of flashes of it keeping lighted up a basic state of ignorance or of half-knowledge and indirect knowledge. As long as it is imperfect, it is invaded by a mixture of ignorant mentality which crosses its truth with a strain of error. After it has acquired a larger native action more free from this intermixture, even then so long as the stuff of mind in which it works is capable of the old intellectual or lower mental habit, it is subject to accretion of error, to clouding, to many kinds of relapse. Moreover the individual mind does not live alone and to itself but in the general mind and all that it has rejected is discharged into the general mind atmosphere around it and tends to return upon and invade it with the old suggestions and many promptings of the old mental character. The intuitive mind, growing or grown, has therefore to be constantly on guard against invasion and accretion, on the watch to reject and eliminate immixtures, busy intuitivising more and still more the whole stuff of mind, and this can only end by itself being enlightened, transformed, lifted up into the full light of the supramental being.[162]

Sri Aurobindo

The way to the intuitive mind

The transformation can be brought about by the removal of the limitation and the elimination of the distorting or perverting element. This however cannot be done by the heightening and greatening of the intellectual activity alone; for that must always be limited by the original inherent defects of the mental intelligence. An intervention of the supramental energy is needed that can light up and get rid of its deficiencies of thought and will and feeling. This intervention too cannot be completely effective unless the supramental plane is manifested and acts above the mind no longer from behind a lid or veil, however thin the veil may have grown, but more constantly in an open and luminous action till there is seen the full sun of Truth with no cloud to moderate its splendour. It is not necessary, either, to develop the intellect fully in its separateness before calling down this intervention or opening up by it the supramental levels. The intervention may come in earlier and at once develop the intellectual action and turn it, as it develops, into the higher intuitive form and substance.

... The most prominent change will be the transmutation of the thought heightened and filled by that substance of concentrated light, concentrated power, concentrated joy of the light and the power and that direct accuracy which are the marks of a true intuitive thinking. It is not only primary suggestions or rapid conclusion that this mind will give, but it will conduct too with the same light, power, joy of sureness and direct spontaneous seeing of the truth the connecting and developing operations now conducted by the intellectual reason. The will also will be changed into this intuitive character, proceed directly with light and power to the thing to be done *kartavyaṁ karma*, and dispose with a rapid sight of possibilities and actualities the combinations necessary to its action and its purpose. The feelings also will be intuitive, seizing upon right relations, acting with a new light and power and a glad sureness, retaining only right and spontaneous desires and emotions, so long as these things endure, and, when they pass away, replacing them by a luminous and spontaneous love and an Ananda that knows and seizes at once on the right *rasa* of its objects. All the other mental movements will be similarly enlightened and even too the pranic and sense movements and the consciousness of the body. And usually there will be some development also of the psychic faculties, powers and perceptions of the inner mind and its senses not dependent on the outer sense and the reason. The intuitive mentality will be not only a stronger and a more luminous thing, but usually capable of a much more extensive operation than the ordinary mind of the same man before this development of the Yoga.[163]

Sri Aurobindo

The intuitive mind

The intuitive mind is an immediate translation of truth into mental terms half transformed by a radiant supramental substance, a translation of some infinite self-knowledge that acts above mind in the superconscient spirit. That spirit becomes conscient to us as a greater self at once above and in and around us of which our present self, our mental, vital and physical personality and nature, is an imperfect portion or a partial derivation or an inferior and inadequate symbol, and as the intuitive mind grows in us, as our whole being grows more moulded to an intuitive substance, we feel a sort of half transformation of our members into the nature of this greater self and spirit. All our thought, will, impulse, feeling, even in the end our more outward vital and physical, sensations become more and more direct transmissions from the spirit and are of another and a more and more pure, untroubled, powerful and luminous nature. This is one side of the change: the other is that whatever belongs still to the lower being, whatever still seems to us to come from outside or as a survival of the action of our old inferior personality, feels the pressure of the change and increasingly tends to modify and transform itself to the new substance and nature. The higher comes down and largely takes the place of the lower, but also the lower changes, transforms itself into material of the action and becomes part of the substance of the higher being.[164]

Sri Aurobindo

The difference between ordinary mind and intuitive mind

The difference between the ordinary mind and the intuitive is that the former, seeking in the darkness or at most by its own unsteady torchlight, first, sees things only as they are presented in that light and, secondly, where it does not know, constructs by imagination, by uncertain inference, by others of its aids and makeshift things which it readily takes for truth, shadow projections, cloud edifices, unreal prolongations, deceptive anticipations, possibilities and probabilities which do duty for certitudes. The intuitive mind constructs nothing in this artificial fashion, but makes itself a receiver of the light and allows the truth to manifest in it and organise its own constructions. But so long as there is a mixed action and the mental constructions and imaginations are allowed to operate, this passivity of the intuitive mind to the higher light, the truth light, cannot be complete or securely dominate and there cannot therefore be a firm organisation of the triple time knowledge. It is because of this obstruction and mixture that that power of time vision, of back-sight and around-sight and foresight, which sometimes marks the illuminated mind, is not only an abnormal power among others rather than part of the very texture of the mental action, but also occasional, very partial and marred often by an undetected intermixture or a self-substituting intervention of error.[165]

Sri Aurobindo

Poetry of the intuitive Mind

A Poet's Stammer

My dream is spoken
    As if by sound
Were tremulously broken
    Some oath profound.

A timeless hush
    Draws ever back
The winging music-rush
    Upon thought's track.

Though syllables sweep
    Like golden birds,
Far lonelihoods of sleep
    Dwindle my words.

Beyond life's clamour,
    A mystery mars
Speech-light to a myriad stammer
    Of flickering stars.

It is a very true and beautiful poem – the subject of the outward stammer seems to be only a starting point or excuse for expressing an inner phenomenon of inspiration. Throughout the inspiration the poem is intuitive.

> [The disciple] You have said before I used to write poems very often from the intuitive mind, but the term you have employed connotes for us the plane between

> the Illumined Mind and the Overmind. But that would be an overhead source of inspiration. Do you mean the intuitivised poetic intelligence? If so, what is its character as compared to the mystic or inner mind?

The intuitive mind, strictly speaking, stretches from the Intuition proper down to the intuitive inner mind – it is therefore at once an overhead power and a mental intelligence power. All depends on the amount, intensity, quality of the intuition and how far it is mixed with mind or pure. The inner mind is not necessarily intuitive, though it can easily become so. The mystic mind is mind turned towards the occult and spiritual, but the inner mind can act without direct reference to the occult and spiritual, it can act in the same field and in the same material as the ordinary mind, only with a larger and deeper power, range and light and in greater unison with the Universal Mind; it can open also more easily to what is within and what is above. Intuitive intelligence, mystic mind, inner mind intelligence are all part of the inner mind operations. In today's poem, for instance, it is certainly the inner mind that has transformed the idea of stammering into a symbol of inner phenomena and into that operation a certain strain of mystic mind enters, but what is prominent is the intuitive inspiration throughout. It starts with the intuitive poetic intelligence in the first stanza, gets touched by the overhead intuition in the second, gets full of it in the third and again rises rapidly to that in the last two lines of the fourth stanza. This is what I call poetry of the intuitive Mind.[166]

Sri Aurobindo

The Overmind is a delegate of the Supermind consciousness

In its nature and law the Overmind is a delegate of the Supermind Consciousness, its delegate to the Ignorance. Or we might speak of it as a protective double, a screen of dissimilar similarity through which Supermind can act indirectly on an Ignorance whose darkness could not bear or receive the direct impact of a supreme Light. Even, it is by the projection of this luminous Overmind corona that the diffusion of a diminished light in the Ignorance and the throwing of that contrary shadow which swallows up in itself all light, the Inconscience, became at all possible. For Supermind transmits to Overmind all its realities, but leaves it to formulate them in a movement and according to an awareness of things which is still a vision of Truth and yet at the same time a first parent of the Ignorance. A line divides Supermind and Overmind which permits a free transmission, allows the lower Power to derive from the higher Power all it holds or sees, but automatically compels a transitional change in the passage. The integrality of the Supermind keeps always the essential truth of things, the total truth and the truth of its individual self-determinations clearly knit together; it maintains in them an inseparable unity and between them a close interpenetration and a free and full consciousness of each other: but in Overmind this integrality is no longer there. And yet the Overmind is well aware of the essential Truth of things; it embraces the totality; it uses the individual self-determinations without being limited by them: but although it knows their oneness, can realise it in a spiritual cognition, yet its dynamic movement, even while relying on that for its security, is not directly determined by it. Overmind Energy proceeds through an illimitable capacity of separation and combination of the powers and aspects of the integral and indivisible all-comprehending Unity. It takes each Aspect or Power and gives to it an independent action in which it acquires a full separate importance and is able to work out, we might say, its own world of creation. Purusha and Prakriti, Conscious Soul and executive Force of Nature, are in the supramental harmony a two-aspected single truth, being and dynamis of the Reality; there can be no disequilibrium or predominance of one over the other. In Overmind we have the origin of the cleavage, the trenchant distinction made by the philosophy of the Sankhyas in which they appear as two independent entities, Prakriti able to dominate Purusha and cloud its freedom and power, reducing it to a witness and recipient of her forms and actions, Purusha able to return to its separate existence and abide in a free self-sovereignty by rejection of her original overclouding material principle. So with the other aspects or powers of the Divine Reality, One and Many, Divine Personality and Divine Impersonality, and the rest; each is still an aspect and power of the one Reality, but each is empowered to act as an independent entity in the whole, arrive at the fullness of the possibilities of its separate expression and develop the dynamic consequences of that separateness. At the same time in Overmind this separateness is still founded on the basis of an implicit underlying unity; all possibilities of combination and relation between the separated Powers and Aspects, all interchanges and mutualities of their energies are freely organised and their actuality always possible.*[167]

Sri Aurobindo

---

* See also the rest of the chapter (pp. 114-148).

The cosmic Mind

But there is possible the attempt to arrive at a kind of cosmic consciousness by dwelling on the lower planes themselves after breaking their limitation laterally, as we have said, and then calling down into them the light and largeness of the higher existence. Not only Spirit is one, but Mind, Life, Matter are one. There is one cosmic Mind, one cosmic Life, one cosmic Body. All the attempt of man to arrive at universal sympathy, universal love and the understanding and knowledge of the inner soul of other existences is an attempt to beat thin, breach and eventually break down by the power of the enlarging mind and heart the walls of the ego and arrive nearer to a cosmic oneness. And if we can by the mind and heart get at the touch of the Spirit, receive the powerful inrush of the Divine into this lower humanity and change our nature into a reflection of the divine nature by love, by universal joy, by oneness of mind with all Nature and all beings, we can break down the walls.[168]

Sri Aurobindo

The Cosmic Spirit

I am a single Self all Nature fills.
   Immeasurable, unmoved the Witness sits:
He is the silence brooding on her hills,
   The circling motion of her cosmic mights.

I have broken the limits of embodied mind
   And am no more the figure of a soul.
The burning galaxies are in me outlined;
   The universe is my stupendous whole.

My life is the life of village and continent,
   I am earth's agony and her throbs of bliss;
I share all creatures' sorrow and content
   And feel the passage of every stab and kiss.

Impassive, I bear each act and thought and mood;
Time traverses my hushed infinitude.[169]

Sri Aurobindo

Opening to the cosmic Mind

Mind has its own realms and life has its own realms just as matter has. In the mental realms life and substance are entirely subordinated to Mind and obey its dictates. Here on earth there is the evolution with matter as the starting-point, life as the medium, mind emerging from it. There are many grades, realms, combinations in the cosmos – there are even many universes. Ours is only one of many.[170]

*

[The results of the opening to the cosmic Mind:] One is aware of the cosmic Mind and the mental forces that move there and how they work on one's mind and that of others and one is able to deal with one's own mind with a greater knowledge and effective power. There are many other results, but this is the fundamental one. This is of course if one opens in the right way and does not merely become a passive field of all sorts of ideas and mental forces.[171]

*

What is happening is that you have got into touch with the cosmic Mind where all sorts of ideas, possibilities, formations are moving about. The individual mind takes up those which appeal to it or perhaps come into distinct form when they touch it. But these are possibilities, not truths, so it is better not to let them run free like that.[172]

Sri Aurobindo

The nature of the action of the cosmic Mind

But Mind by its very nature tends to know and sense substance of conscious-being, not in its unity or totality but by the principle of division. It sees it, as it were, in infinitesimal points which it associates together in order to arrive at a totality, and into these viewpoints and associations cosmic Mind throws itself and dwells in them. So dwelling, creative by its inherent force as the agent of Real-Idea, bound by its own nature to convert all its perceptions into energy of life, as the All-Existent converts all His self-aspectings into various energy of His creative Force of consciousness, cosmic Mind turns these, its multiple viewpoints of universal existence, into standpoints of universal Life; it turns them in Matter into forms of atomic being instinct with the life that forms them and governed by the mind and will that actuate the formation. At the same time, the atomic existences which it thus forms must by the very law of their being tend to associate themselves, to aggregate; and each of these aggregates also, instinct with the hidden life that forms and the hidden mind and will that actuate them, bears with it a fiction of a separated individual existence. Each such individual object or existence is supported, according as the mind in it is implicit or explicit, unmanifest or manifest, by its mechanical ego of force, in which the will-to-be is dumb and imprisoned but none the less powerful, or by its self-aware mental ego in which the will-to-be is liberated, conscious, separately active.

Thus not any eternal and original law of eternal and original Matter, but the nature of the action of cosmic Mind is the cause of atomic existence. Matter is a creation, and for its creation the infinitesimal, an extreme fragmentation of the Infinite, was needed as the starting-point or basis. Ether may and does exist as an intangible, almost spiritual support of Matter, but as a phenomenon it does not seem, to our present knowledge at least, to be materially detectable.[173]

Sri Aurobindo

The universal Mind

But still the question remains why Energy should take the form of Matter and not of mere force-currents or why that which is really Spirit should admit the phenomenon of Matter and not rest in states, velleities and joys of the spirit. This, it is said, is the work of Mind or else, since evidently Thought does not directly create or even perceive the material form of things, it is the work of Sense; the sense-mind creates the forms which it seems to perceive and the thought-mind works upon the forms which the sense-mind presents to it. But, evidently, the individual embodied mind is not the creator of the phenomenon of Matter; earth-existence cannot be the result of the human mind which is itself the result of earth-existence. If we say that the world exists only in our own minds, we express a non-fact and a confusion; for the material world existed before man was upon the earth and it will go on existing if man disappears from the earth or even if our individual mind abolishes itself in the Infinite. We must conclude then that there is a universal Mind, subconscious to us in the form of the universe or superconscious in its spirit, which has created that form for its habitation. And since the creator must have preceded and must exceed its creation, this really implies a superconscient Mind which by the instrumentality of a universal sense creates* in itself the relation of form with form and constitutes the rhythm of the material universe. But this also is no complete solution; it tells us that Matter is a creation of Consciousness, but it does not explain how Consciousness came to create Matter as the basis of its cosmic workings.[174]

Sri Aurobindo

The ranges above Mind in universal Mind

In universal Mind itself there are ranges above our mentality which are instruments of the cosmic truth-cognition, and into these the mental being can surely rise; for already it rises towards them in supernormal conditions or receives from them without yet knowing or possessing them intuitions, spiritual intimations, large influxes of illumination or spiritual capacity. All these ranges are conscious of what is beyond them, and the highest of them is directly open to the Supermind, aware of the Truth-Consciousness which exceeds it. Moreover, in the evolving being itself, those greater powers of consciousness are here, supporting Mind-truth, underlying its action which screens them; this Supermind and those

---

*Mind, as we know it, creates only in a relative and instrumental sense; it has an unlimited power of combination, but its creative motives and forms come to it from above: all created forms have their base in the Infinite above Mind, Life and Matter and are here represented, reconstructed – are very usually misconstructed – from the infinitesimal. Their foundation is above, their branchings downwards, says the Rig Veda. The superconscient Mind of which we speak might rather be called an Overmind and inhabits in the hierarchical order of the powers of the Spirit, a zone directly dependent on the supramental consciousness. (Sri Aurobindo)

Truth-powers uphold Nature by their secret presence: even, truth of Mind is their result, a diminished operation, a representation in partial figures. It is, therefore, not only natural but seems inevitable that these higher powers of Existence should manifest here in Mind as Mind itself has manifested in Life and Matter.[175]

Sri Aurobindo

The universal Mind around us

Around us is a universal Mind of which our mind is a formation and our thoughts, feelings, will, impulses are continually little more than a personally modified reception and transcription of its thought-waves, its force-currents, its foam of emotion and sensation, its billows of impulse.[176]

Sri Aurobindo

The working of the forces of the universal Mind

We begin to perceive the working of the forces of universal Mind and to know how our thoughts are created by that working, separate from within the truth and falsehood of our perceptions, enlarge their field, extent and illumine their significance, become master of our own minds and active to shape the movements of Mind in the world around us. We begin to perceive the flow and surge of the universal life-forces, detect the origin and law of our feelings, emotions, sensations, passions, are free to accept, reject, new-create, rise to higher planes of Life-Power. We begin to perceive too the key to the enigma of Matter, follow the interplay of Mind and Life and Consciousness upon it, discover more and more its instrumental and resultant function and detect ultimately the last secret of Matter as a form not merely of Energy but of involved and arrested or unstably fixed and restricted consciousness and begin to see too the possibility of its liberation and plasticity of response to higher Powers, its possibilities for the conscious and no longer the more than half-inconscient incarnation and self-expression of the Spirit. All this and more becomes more and more possible as the working of the Divine Shakti increases in us and, against much resistance or labour to respond of our obscure consciousness, through much struggle and movement of progress and regression and renewed progress necessitated by the work of intensive transformation of a half-inconscient into a conscious substance, moves to a greater purity, truth, height, range. All depends on the psychic awakening in us, the completeness of our response to her and our growing surrender.[177]

Sri Aurobindo

How thoughts are created by the forces of the universal Mind

Because the forces of the universal Mind enter into our heads. We are bathed in forces, we are not aware of it. We are not something enclosed in a bag and independent from the rest; all forces, all vibrations, all movements enter into us and pass through us. And so we have a certain mental force held in, that is to say, ready to be used by the formative or creative mental power. These are, as it were, free forces. As soon as a thought coming from outside or a force or a movement enters our consciousness, we give it a concrete form, a logical appearance and all kinds of precise details; but in fact all this belongs to a domain one is rarely conscious of.

But this is not a special instance which occurs only from

time to time: it is something constant. If a current of force is passing, with a particular thought formation, one sees it passing from one into another, and in each one it forms as a kind of centre of light or force which keeps the imprint – more or less pure, more or less clear, more or less mixed – of the initial current; and the result is what we call "our" thought.

But our thought is something which hardly exists. It can be "our" thought only if, instead of being like a public place as we generally are in our normal state – we are like a public place and all the forces pass there, come and go, enter, depart, jostle each other and even quarrel – if instead of being like that, we are a concentrated consciousness, turned upwards in an aspiration, and open beyond the limits of the human mind to something higher; then, being open like this brings down that higher something across all the layers of reality, and this something may enter into contact with our conscious brain and take a form there which is no longer the creation of a universal force or a personal mind stronger than ours, but the *direct* expression and creation of a light which is above us, and which may be a light of the highest kind if our aspiration and opening allow it. That is the only case in which one can say that the thought is our own. ...

How is the thought formed in the universal Mind?

...There is a region of the mind, higher than the ordinary mind, in which there are ideas, typal ideas, really prototypes; and these ideas descend and are clothed in mental substance. So, in accordance with – how to put it? – the quality of the receiver, they either keep all their own qualities and original nature or become distorted, coloured, transformed in the individual consciousness. But the idea goes far beyond the

Towards Supermind

mind; the idea has an origin much higher than the mind. So, the functioning is the same from both the universal and the individual point of view; the individual movement is only representative of the universal one. The *scale* is different, but the phenomenon is the same. Of course, these are no longer "thoughts" as we conceive thoughts; they are universal principles – but it's the same thing – universal principles on which the universes are built.

The universe, after all, is only one person, only one individuality in the midst of the eternal Creation. Each universe is a person, who takes form, lives, dissolves, and another takes shape – it is the same thing. For us, the person is the human individual; and from the universal point of view the person is the universal individual; it is one universe in the midst of all the universes.*[178]

The Mother

---

* See also **Appendix** *How to think* (Ed. Note)

BEYOND MIND: THE SUPERMIND

BEYOND MIND: THE SUPERMIND

Supermind is beyond mind, life and Matter

Supermind is the grade of existence beyond mind, life and Matter and, as mind, life and Matter have manifested on the earth, so too must Supermind in the inevitable course of things manifest in this world of Matter. In fact, a supermind is already here but it is involved, concealed behind this manifest mind, life and Matter and not yet acting overtly or in its own power: if it acts, it is through these inferior powers and modified by their characters and so not yet recognisable. It is only by the approach and arrival of the descending Supermind that it can be liberated upon earth and reveal itself in the action of our material, vital and mental parts so that these lower powers can become portions of a total divinised activity of our whole being: it is that that will bring to us a completely realised divinity or the divine life. It is indeed so that life and mind involved in Matter have realised themselves here; for only what is involved can evolve, otherwise there could be no emergence.[179]

Sri Aurobindo

---

* brought

Transformation

My breath runs in a subtle rhythmic stream;
   It fills my members with a might divine:
     I have drunk the Infinite like a giant's wine.
Time is my drama or my pageant dream.
Now are my illumined cells joy's flaming scheme
   And changed my thrilled and branching nerves to fine
     Channels of rapture opal and hyaline
For the influx of the Unknown and the Supreme.

I am no more a vassal of the flesh,
   A slave to Nature and her leaden rule;
I am caught no more in the senses' narrow mesh.
My soul unhorizoned widens to measureless sight,
   My body is God's happy living tool,
My spirit a vast sun of deathless light.[180]

                                      Sri Aurobindo

The mind of Light

A new humanity means for us the appearance, the development of a type or race of mental beings whose principle of mentality would be no longer a mind in the Ignorance seeking for knowledge but even in its knowledge bound to the Ignorance, a seeker after Light but not its natural possessor, open to the Light but not an inhabitant of the Light, not yet a perfected instrument, truth-conscious and delivered out of the Ignorance. Instead, it would be possessed already of what could be called a mind of Light, a mind capable of living in the truth, capable of being truth-conscious and manifesting in its life a direct in place of an indirect knowledge. Its mentality would be an instrument of the Light and no longer of the Ignorance. At its highest it would be capable of passing into the supermind and from the new race would be recruited the race of supramental beings who would appear as the leaders of the evolution in earth-nature. Even, the highest manifestations of a mind of Light would be an instrumentality of the supermind, a part of it or a projection from it, a stepping beyond humanity into the superhumanity of the supramental principle. Above all, its possession would enable the human being to rise beyond the normalities of his present thinking, feeling and being into those highest powers of the mind in its self-exceedings which intervene between our mentality and supermind and can be regarded as steps leading towards the greater and more luminous principle.[181]

... It is in this series of the order of existence and as the last word of the lower hemisphere of being, the first word of the higher hemisphere that we have to look at the Mind of Light and see what is its nature and the powers which characterise it and which it uses for its self-manifestation and workings, its connection with the Supermind and its consequences and possibilities for the life of a new humanity.[182]

Sri Aurobindo

The Supermind is Truth-Cconsciousness

A Divine life upon earth, the ideal we have placed before us, can only come about by a spiritual change of our being and a radical and fundamental change, an evolution or revolution of our nature. The embodied being upon earth would have to rise out of the domination over it of its veils of mind, life and body into the full consciousness and possession of its spiritual reality and its nature also would have to be lifted out of the consciousness and power of consciousness proper to mental, vital and physical being into the greater consciousness and greater power of being and the larger and freer life of the spirit... This ... could not be if mind, life and body were not taken up and transformed by a state of being and a force of being superior to them, a power of Supermind as much above our incomplete mental nature as that is above the nature of animal life and animated Matter, as it is immeasurably above the mere material nature.

The Supermind is in its very essence a truth-consciousness, a consciousness always free from the Ignorance which is the foundation of our present natural or evolutionary existence and from which nature in us is trying to arrive at self-knowledge and world-knowledge and a right consciousness and the right use of our existence in the universe. The Supermind, because it is a truth-consciousness, has this knowledge inherent in it and this power of true existence; its course is straight and can go direct to its aim, its field is wide and can even be made illimitable... On its summits it possesses the divine omniscience and omnipotence, but even in an evolutionary movement of its own graded self-manifestation by which it would eventually reveal its own highest heights it must be in its very nature essentially free from ignorance and error, it starts from truth and light and moves always in truth and light.[183]

Sri Aurobindo

The forerunners of a divine multitude

I saw the Omnipotent's flaming pioneers
Over the heavenly verge which turns towards life
Come crowding down the amber stairs of birth;
Forerunners of a divine multitude,
Out of the paths of the morning star they came
Into the little room of mortal life.
I saw them cross the twilight of an age,
The sun-eyed children of a marvelous dawn,
The great creators with wide brows of calm,
The massive barrier-breakers of the world
And wrestlers with destiny in her lists of will,
The labourers in the quarries of the gods,
The messengers of the Incommunicable,
The architects of immortality.
In the fallen human sphere they came,
Faces that wore the Immortal's glory still,
Voices that communed with the thoughts of God,
Bodies made beautiful by the spirit's light,
Carrying the magic word, the mystic fire,
Carrying the Dionysian cup of joy,
Approaching eyes of a diviner man,
Lips chanting an unknown anthem of the soul,
Feet echoing in the corridors of Time.
High priests of wisdom, sweetness, might and bliss,
Discoverers of beauty's sunlit ways
And swimmers of Love's laughing fiery floods

Beyond Mind: the Supermind

And dancers within rapture's golden doors,
Their tread one day shall change the suffering earth
And justify the light on Nature's face.

....

This high divine successor surely shall come

....

He shall know what mortal mind barely durst think,
He shall do what the heart of the mortal could not dare.

....

Earth's deeds shall touch the superhuman's height,
Earth's seeing widen into the infinite.[184]

Sri Aurobindo

Supermind: the experience of the supreme Infinite

But if we can once cross beyond the Mind's frontier twilight into the vast plane of supramental Knowledge, these devices cease to be indispensable. Supermind has quite another, a positive and direct and living experience of the supreme Infinite. The Absolute is beyond personality and beyond impersonality, and yet it is both the Impersonal and the supreme Person and all persons. The Absolute is beyond the distinction of unity and multiplicity, and yet it is the One and the innumerable Many in all the universe. It is beyond all limitation by quality and yet it is not limited by a qualityless void but is too all infinite qualities. It is the individual soul and all souls and none of them; it is the formless Brahman and the universe. It is the cosmic and the supracosmic Spirit, the supreme Lord, the supreme Self, the supreme Purusha and supreme Shakti, the Ever Unborn who is endlessly born, the Infinite who is innumerably finite, the multitudinous One, the complex Simple, the many-sided Single, the Word of the Silence Ineffable, the impersonal omnipresent Person, the Mystery, translucent in highest consciousness to its own spirit, but to a lesser consciousness veiled in its own exceeding light and impenetrable for ever. These things are to the dimensional mind irreconcilable opposites, but to the constant vision and experience of the supramental Truth-Consciousness they are so simply and inevitably the intrinsic nature of each other that even to think of them as contraries is an unimaginable violence. The walls constructed by the measuring and separating Intellect have disappeared and the Truth in its simplicity and beauty appears and reduces all to terms of its harmony and unity and light. Dimensions and distinctions remain but as figures for use, not a separative prison for the self-forgetting Spirit.

The consciousness of the transcendent Absolute with its consequence in individual and universe is the last, the eternal knowledge.[185]

Sri Aurobindo

To become the divine superman

This is thy work and the aim of thy being and that for which thou art here, to become the divine superman and a perfect vessel of the Godhead. All else that thou hast to do, is only a making thyself ready or a joy by the way or a fall from the purpose. But the goal is this and the purpose is this and not in power of the way and the joy by the way but in the joy of the goal is the greatness and the delight of thy being. The joy of the way is because that which is drawing thee is also with thee on thy path and the power to climb was given thee that thou mightiest mount to thy own summits.

If thou hast a duty, this is thy duty; if thou ask what shall be thy aim, let this be thy aim; if thou demand pleasure, there is no greater joy, for all other joy is broken or limited, the joy of a dream or the joy of a sleep or the joy of self-forgetting. But this is the joy of thy whole being. For if thou say what is thy being, this is thy being, the Divine, and all else is only its broken or its perverse appearance. If thou seek the Truth, this is the Truth. Place it before thee and in all things be faithful to it.

It has been well said by one who saw but through a veil and mistook the veil for the face, that thy aim is to become thyself; and he said well again that the nature of man is to transcend himself. This is indeed his nature and that is indeed the divine aim of his self-transcending.

What then is the self that thou hast to transcend and what is the self that thou hast to become? For it is here that thou shouldst make no error; for this error, not to know thyself, is the fountain of all thy grief and the cause of all thy stumbling.

That which thou hast to transcend is the self that thou appearest to be, and that is man as thou knowest him, the apparent Purusha. And what is this man? He is a mental being enslaved to life and matter; and where he is not enslaved to life and matter, he is the slave of his mind. But this is a great and heavy servitude; for to be the slave of mind is to be the slave of the false, the limited and the apparent. The self that thou hast to become, is that self that thou art within behind the veil of mind, and life and matter. It is to be the spiritual, the divine, the superman, the real Purusha. For that which is above the mental being, is the superman. It is to be the master of thy mind, thy life and thy body; it is to be a king over Nature of whom thou art now the tool, lifted above her who now has thee under her feet. It is to be free and not a slave, to be one and not divided, to be immortal and not obscured by death, to be full of light and not darkened, to be full of bliss and not the sport of grief and suffering, to be uplifted into power and not cast down into weakness. It is to live in the Infinite and possess the finite. It is to live in God and be one with him in his being. To become thyself is to be this and all that flows from it.

Be free in thyself, and therefore free in thy mind, free in thy life and thy body. For the Spirit is freedom.

Be one with God and all beings; live in thyself and not in thy little ego. For the Spirit is unity.

Be thyself, immortal, and put not thy faith in death; for death is not of thyself, but of thy body. For the Spirit is immortality.

Beyond Mind: the Supermind

To be immortal is to be infinite in being and consciousness and bliss; for the Spirit is infinite and that which is finite lives only by his infinity.

These things thou art, therefore thou canst become all these; but if thou wert not these things, then thou couldst never become them. What is within thee, that alone can be revealed in thy being. Thou appearest indeed to be other than this, but wherefore shouldst thou enslave thyself to appearances?

Rather arise, transcend thyself, become thyself. Thou art man and the whole nature of man is to become more than himself. He was the man-animal, he has become more than the animal man. He is the thinker, the craftsman, the seeker after beauty. He shall be more than the thinker, he shall be the seer of knowledge; he shall be more than the craftsman, he shall be the creator and master of his creation; he shall be more than the seeker of beauty, for he shall enjoy all beauty and all delight. Physical he seeks for his immortal substance; vital he seeks after immortal life and the infinite power of his being; mental and partial in knowledge, he seeks after the whole light and the utter vision.

To possess these is to become the superman; for [it] is to rise out of mind into the supermind. Call it the divine mind or Knowledge or the supermind; it is the power and light of the divine will and the divine consciousness. By the supermind the Spirit saw and created himself in the worlds, by that he lives in them and governs them. By that he is Swarat Samrat, self-ruler and all ruler.

Supermind is superman; therefore to rise beyond mind is the condition.

To be the superman is to live the divine life, to be a god, for the gods are the powers of God. Be a power of God in humanity.

To live in the divine Being and let the consciousness and bliss, the will and knowledge of the Spirit possess thee and play with thee and through thee, this is the meaning.

This is the transfiguration of thyself on the mountain. It is to discover God in thyself and reveal him to thyself in all things. Live in his being, shine with his light, act with his power, rejoice with his bliss. Be that Fire and that Sun and that Ocean. Be that joy, that greatness and that beauty.

When thou hast done this even in part, thou hast attained to the first steps of supermanhood.[186]

Sri Aurobindo

APPENDIX

THE VARIOUS MINDS IN *SAVITRI*

In *Savitri,* we have not only Sri Aurobindo's full description of his yoga but also his experience of many more minds and mind states than are included within the Minds Levels described in our selections.

The references of the Minds listed below are taken from the final edition of *Savitri* first issued in 1993. Each reference indicates the page number, the line number mentioning a given mind. For example, the reference to *waking mind* is page 347, line 15; it is listed below in this way:

347: 15 Collapsed to *waking mind.* Eternity

* brought

The Hierarchy of Minds

SURFACE MIND – Outward Mind, Waking Mind, Sceptic Mind, Infant Mind, Covering Mind, Half-Conscious Mind, Outer Mind, Common Mind.

  27: 29 A world unseen, unknown by *outward mind**
  49: 27 Else to our *waking mind*'s small moment look
 156: 13 Awaited life and sense and *waking Mind.*
 170: 21 Even in our *sceptic mind* of ignorance
 257: 7 In this small mould of *infant mind* and sense
 293: 29 By the *outward mind* unrecognisable,
 319: 11 The *covering mind* was seized and torn apart;
 241: 30 In the vague light of man's *half-conscious mind*,
 347: 15 Collapsed to *waking mind.* Eternity
 395: 1 Wandering unwarned by the slow *surface mind*,
 500: 23 And pass through masked doorways into *outer mind*
 539: 1 Affranchised from the look of *surface mind*
 540: 11 But for the mortal prisoned in *outward mind*
 541: 32 This too she saw that all in *outer mind*
 563: 5 Their thoughts which to the *common mind* are blank
 622: 24 In *waking Mind* the Thinker built his house.
 689: 15 The doors of light are sealed to *common mind*,

SUBLIMINAL MIND – Occult Mind, Bright Mind, Mastering Mind, Inmost Mind, Unsleeping Mind, Inner Mind, Hidden Mind, Dream-Mind, Inner Seeing Mind.

  39: 22 Passed through the masked office of the *occult mind*,
  74: 2 Admitted through a curtain of *bright mind*
  83: 22 Confessed the advent of a *mastering Mind*
  88: 26 Was hung upon a wall of *inmost mind.*

* Italics are ours. (Ed.)

96:	19	The exhaustless seeings of the *unsleeping Mind*,
117:	8	As saw some *inner mind,* so life was shaped:
147:	3	Could never have disclosed its *hidden mind,*
153:	11	The veiled suggesions of a *hidden Mind*
178:	36	It dared to trust the *dream-mind* and the soul.
268:	34	Their mind could penetrate her *occult mind*
407:	25	I plunged into an *inner seeing Mind*
485:	13	Our *inner Mind* dwells in a larger light,
503:	9	She looked out far and saw from *inner mind*
540:	16	Only to the *inner mind* they speak direct,

PHYSICAL MIND - Earthly Mind, Corporeal Mind, Terrestrial Mind, Corner-Mind, Embodied Mind, Early Mind, Earth-Mind, Material Mind, Mind of Flesh, Mind of Earth, Earth-Mind, Sleeping Mind, Body's Mind, Bodily Mind, Fixed Mind, Matter's Mind, Slumbering Mind.

32:	19	His centre was no more in *earthly mind;*
55:	4	And man's *corporeal mind* is the only lamp,
104:	7	It shields our ceiling of *terrestrial mind*
114:	25	Assigned as Force to a bound *corner-Mind*
116:	3	He crossed the limits of *embodied Mind*
146:	30	A mould of body's *early mind* was made.
178:	34	It lingered not like the *earth-mind* hemmed in
232:	7	The wisdom *embodied mind* could not reveal,
240:	4	The slow process of a *material mind*
242:	1	Cut sentient passages for the *mind of flesh*
243:	14	Its young formations move the *mind of earth*
281:	6	Impoverished not by *earth-mind*'s indigence,
302:	3	Thoughts rose in him no *earthly mind* can hold,
360:	28	Upraised the *earth-mind* to superhuman heights.
398:	10	His instrument the dim *corporeal mind,*

443: 22 Awoke to itself the dreamer, *sleeping Mind;*
456: 32 How shall my voice convince the *mind of earth?*
489: 6 That bars out from our depths the *body's mind*
491: 25 The press of *bodily mind,* the Inconscient's brood
498: 5 Here was a quiet country of *fixed mind,*
565: 6 Only the dull and *physical mind* was left,
572: 2 And godlike thoughts surprise the *mind of earth.*
615: 20 All thy high dreams were made by *Matter's mind*
650: 7 The *earth-mind* sinks and it despairs and looks
688: 12 Heaven's light visits sometimes the *mind of earth;*
699: 6 The *mind of earth* shall be a home of light,
710: 27 Lighting the chambers of the *slumbering mind;*

VITAL MIND – Animal Mind, Life-Mind, Mind of Life, Life Mind.

 53: 16 Inheritor of the brief *animal mind.*
148: 7 It fashioned the *life-mind* of bird and beast,
162: 11 A thinking puppet is the *mind of life:*
249: 4 Instinct its dam and the *life-mind* its sire,
622: 15 In a subconscient *Life Mind* lay asleep;

MENTAL MIND – Conscious Mind, Thinking Mind, Schoolman Mind, Thought-Mind, Measuring Mind, Interpreting Mind.

132: 26 Dividing Matter's sleep from *conscious Mind,*
158: 13 A *thinking mind* had come to lift life's moods,
259: 15 A pure *Thought-Mind* surveyed the cosmic act.
320: 30 Transgressing the dream-shores of *conscious Mind*
348: 4 And toiled with the form-maker, *measuring Mind.*
404: 27 Were seen anew through the *interpreting mind*

Appendix

484: 25 It sees from summits beyond *thinking mind*,
496: 4 A *schoolman mind* had captured life's large space,
511: 22 His *conscious mind* her strong revolted serf.
529: 11 Which *thinking mind* has made its busy space,
625: 26 A crooked maze they made of *thinking mind*,
626: 25 It makes a cloud of the *interpreting mind*
645: 29 A legend told to itself by *conscious Mind*,

SPIRITUAL MIND – Overmind, Seeing Mind, Ideal Mind, Illumined Mind, Visionary Mind, Summit Mind.

 41: 12 Above the golden *Overmind's* shimmering ridge.
 83: 35 The prophet passion of a *seeing Mind*.
260: 27 The splendours of *ideal Mind* were seen
277: 21 The heavens of the *ideal Mind* were seen
302: 5 He scanned the secrets of the *Overmind*,
317: 28 Secret, unnoted by the *illumined mind*,
606: 1 Seen hardly by a *visionary mind*,
650: 10 At last he wakes into *spiritual mind;*
659: 26 On *summit Mind* are radiant altitudes
660: 24 The cosmic empire of the *Overmind*,
677: 33 There breath carried a stream of *seeing mind*,
694: 13 And not on the luminous peaks of *summit Mind*,

UNIVERSAL MIND – Cosmic Mind, Multitudinous Mind, Eternal Mind, Mind of Space.

 40: 8 The magician order of the *cosmic Mind*
 75: 29 Once more was heard in the still *cosmic Mind*
 88: 34 Then glad of a glory of *multitudinous mind*
109: 1 A thought from the *eternal Mind* draws near,
221: 13 Inconscience swallowing up the *cosmic Mind*,

250: 26 Coercing the plastic stuff of *cosmic Mind*.
299: 34 He rode the lightning seas of *cosmic Mind*
308: 2 Nothing remained the *cosmic Mind* conceives.
351: 9 A dream loitered in the dumb *mind of Space,*
427: 2 The eternal poet, *universal Mind.*
565: 25 Had taken a sensible form. *A cosmic mind*

SUPERMIND – Truth Mind, Mind of Light.

121: 15 At her will the inscrutable *Supermind* leans down
187: 32 Out of the secret *Supermind's* huge store.
357: 14 *A mind of light,* a life of rhythmic force,
661: 36 In the realms of the immortal *Supermind*
705: 27 Eternal *supermind* touch earthly Time.
706: 24 The *supermind* shall be his nature's fount,
707: 12 The *supermind* shall claim the world for Light

OTHER ASPECTS OF MIND-LEVELS

LIMITLESS MIND – Immortal Mind, God-Mind, Infinite Mind, Infinite Mind-space, Silent Mind.

262: 25 An errant ray from the *immortal Mind*
280: 16 Through a pale-sapphire ether of *god-mind*
346: 7 A *limitless Mind* that can contain the world,
394: 10 His mind was open to her *infinite mind.*
479: 11 Adventuring into *infinite mind-space*
546: 24 Was a design sketched on a *silent mind*
660: 36 And there the boundaries of *immortal Mind:*
675: 29 Were here the first lexicon of an *infinite mind*

SEEKING MIND – Dwarf-search Mind, Groping Mind, Seeing Mind, Explorer Mind, Seeking Mind, Divining Mind, All-seeking Mind, All-seeing Mind, Listening Mind.

- 58: 10 Our *dwarf-search mind* to meet the Omniscient's light
- 68: 13 And veils his knowledge by the *groping mind.*
- 83: 35 The prophet-passion of a *seeing Mind.*
- 87: 31 There tirelessly tempted the *explorer mind*
- 109: 20 Here is man's ignorant *divining mind,*
- 223: 8 A *seeking Mind* replaced the seeing Soul:
- 250: 17 Ignorant of all but her own *seeking mind.*
- 292: 8 And the unanimity of *seeing minds*
- 319: 27 His *seeking mind* ceased in the Truth that knows;
- 380: 20 The quieted *all-seeking mind* could feel,
- 407: 25 I plunged into an inner *seeing Mind*
- 421: 5 His *listening mind* had marked the dubious close,
- 555: 24 It was sight and thought in one *all-seeing Mind*,
- 677: 33 There breath carried a stream of *seeing mind*,

VOICEFUL MIND -- Expressing Mind

- 283: 29 Into the *voiceful mind*, the labouring world;
- 529: 15 Where speech must rise and the *expressing mind*

HUMAN MIND -- Mortal Mind, Mind of Man, Man's Mind.

- 6: 19 The call that wakes the leap of *human mind,*
- 35: 35 Widening the *mortal mind's* half-look on things,
- 42: 24 Than what the slow labour of *human mind* can bring,
- 48: 6 In the oblivious field of *mortal mind*,
- 99: 1 Lifts *mortal mind* into a greater air,
- 105: 1 Figures are there undreamed by *mortal mind*:

The Hierarchy of Minds

168: 26 It labours in our *mortal mind* and sense;
260: 3 For Thought transcends the circles of *mortal mind*,
261: 30 Closed to the uncertain thoughts of *human mind*.
264: 35 The first realms were close and kin to *human mind;*
265: 19 Interpreters between *man's mind* and God's,
274: 8 There must she dwell mured in the *human mind*,
276: 4 The vanity of our shut *mortal mind*
306: 34 And *human mind* must abdicate in Light
339: 17 However *man's mind* may tire or fail his flesh,
344: 28 He shall know what *mortal mind* barely durst think,
353: 9 Bridging the gulf between *man's mind* and God's;
370: 26 And feel the breaking walls of *mortal mind*
406: 17 And moved my *mortal mind* shall understand
407: 15 Hoping to fix its rule by *mortal mind*,
437: 16 Awhile she fell to the level of *human mind*,
444: 15 Against the deep folly of his *human mind*,
457: 36 Yet can the *mind of man* receive God's light,
484: 13 Lit by the uncertain ray of *human mind*,
488: 20 Only if God assumes the *human mind*
510: 7 I break the ignorant pride of *human mind*
516: 20 But *human mind* clings to its ignorance,
516: 32 *Man's mind* shall admit the sovereignty of Truth
516: 36 A voice of the sense-shackled *human mind*
520: 35 The *mind of man* will think it earth's own gleam,
607: 10 The subtle marvellous *mind of man* has feigned,
608: 17 O *human mind*, vainly thou torturest
618: 7 In the tangled pathways of the *human mind*,
618: 14 A magnified image of *man's mind* for God,
648: 28 How sayst thou Truth can never light the *human mind*
690: 19 The Inconscient could not read without *man's mind*

Appendix

LIMITING MIND – Bounded Mind, Sceptic Mind, Covering Mind, Tangled Mind, Severing Mind, Costuming Mind, Earth-bound Mind.

  25: 33 The *bounded mind* became a boundless light,
  64: 24 And the creative error of *limiting mind*
170: 21 Even in our *sceptic mind* of ignorance
319: 11 The *covering mind* was seized and torn apart;
512: 31 Out of a *tangled mind* and half-made soul
657: 1 In Light are joined, but sundered by *severing Mind*
677: 15 Deformed by our search, tricked by *costuming mind*,
693: 34 Across the last confines of the *limiting Mind*
705: 23 The great deliverers of *earth-bound mind*,

MIND OF NIGHT – Subconscious Mind, Unremembering Mind, Sleeping Mind, Subterranean Mind, Darkened Mind, Slumbering Mind

    1: 3 The huge foreboding *mind of Night*, alone
161: 33 The troglodytes of the *subconscious Mind*,
290: 2 But nameless to the *unremembering mind*,
443: 22 Awoke to itself the dreamer, *sleeping Mind*;
483: 30 And nothing checked by *subterranean mind*,
710: 9 And even *darkened mind* quiver with new life
710: 27 Lighting the chambers of the *slumbering mind*;

HOW TO THINK

*You have asked the teachers "to think with **ideas** instead of with words." You have also said that later on you will ask them to think with **experiences**. Will you throw some light on these three ways of thinking?*

Our house has a very high tower; at the very top of that tower there is a bright and bare room, the last one before we emerge into the open air, into the full light.

Sometimes, when we are at leisure to do so, we climb up to this bright room, and there, if we remain very quiet, one or more visitors call on us; some are tall, others small, some single, others in groups, all are bright and graceful.

Usually, in our joy at their arrival and in our haste to receive them well, we lose our tranquility and come galloping down to rush into the large hall which forms the base of the tower and which is the store-room of words. Here, more or less excited, we select, reject, assemble, combine, disarrange, rearrange all the words within our reach in an attempt to transcribe this or that visitor who has come to us. But most often the picture we succeed in making of her is more like a caricature than a portrait.

And yet if we were wiser, we would remain up there at the summit of the tower, quite still, in joyful contemplation. Then, after a certain length of time, we would see the visitors themselves descending slowly, gracefully, calmly, without losing anything of their elegance or beauty and, as they cross the store-room of words, clothing themselves effortlessly, automatically, with the words needed to make them perceptible even in the material house.

This is what I call thinking with ideas...

31 May 1960

Appendix

When you think with words, you can express what you think with those words only. To think with ideas is to be able to put the same idea in many kinds of words. The words can also be of different languages, if you happen to know more than one language. This is the first, the most elementary thing about thinking with ideas.

When you think with experience, you go much deeper and you can express the same experience with many kinds of ideas. Then thought can take this form or that form in any language and through all of them the essential realisation will remain unchanged.[187]

The Mother

GLOSSARY

GLOSSARY

Absolute, the
The supreme reality of that transcendent being which we call God. The ineffable x overtopping and underlying and immanent and essential in all of that we call existence or non-existence.*

ahankara
Ego-sense; ego-idea; the separative ego-sense which makes each being conceive of itself as an independent personality.

Ananda
Bliss; delight; the essential principle of delight.

antahkarana
The inner instrument; the sum total of the faculties of Mind; mind and vital as opposed to the body.

Ashram
The house of the Master (*guru*); a spiritual retreat or community, for practising a yogic and spiritual discipline.

Atman
The spiritual being above the mind; the Self or Spirit that remains above, pure and stainless, unaffected by the stains of life, by desire and ego and ignorance. It is realised as the true being of the individual, but also more widely as the *same being* in all and as the Self in the cosmos.

Being
Pure Being is the affirmation by the Unknowable of It-

---

* Most definitions are taken directly from Sri Aurobindo's writings, especially from *The Life Divine*, *The Synthesis of Yoga*, and *Letters on Yoga*.

self as the free base of all cosmic existence.

Bhakti Yoga

The Yoga of Devotion.

bhoga

Enjoyment; possession.

Body

Matter; body is only a mass of force of consciousness being employed as a starting-point for the variable relations of consciousness working through its power of sense.

Brahman

The Absolute; the supreme Reality that is one and indivisible and infinite, besides which nothing else really exists. It is individual and universal as well as transcendental.

buddhi

The intelligence; the intelligent will; the instrument of thought; the mental power of understanding in classical Indian psychology.

chaitya puruṣa

The psychic being: the individual soul or spark of the Divine. When the soul or spark of the Divine Fire begins to develop a psychic personality, that psychic individuality is called the psychic being. The soul is something of the Divine that descends into the evolution of the individual out of Ignorance into Light. This individuality grows from life to life, using the evolving mind, vital and body as its instruments. It is the soul, the psychic that is immortal.

Chitta (*citta*)

The stuff of mixed mental-vital-physical consciousness

out of which arise the movements of thought, emotion, sensation, impulse etc.

Consciousness

The self-aware power of existence. Consciousness is not only power of awareness of self and things, it is or has also a dynamic and creative energy. It can determine its own reactions or abstain from reactions; it can not only answer to forces, but create or put out from itself forces. Consciousness is not synonymous with mentality, which is only a middle term; below mentality it sinks into vital and material movements which are for us subconscient; above, it rises into the supramental which is for us the superconscient. But in all it is one and the same thing, organising itself differently.

Divine, the

The Supreme Being from whom all have come and in whom all are. In its supreme Truth the Divine is absolute and infinite peace, consciousness, existence, power and delight.

Ego

The separative sense of individuality. The ego of the mind, vital and body is bent on self-affirmation and used by the vital urge for its life-desire and life-purpose. The surface mental individuality is egocentric: it looks at the world and things and happenings from its own standpoint and sees them not as they are but as they affect itself. At the same time, the ego is the first indispensable step of individualisation, and that which separates "I" from everything else. When it is fully formed, it must surrender to the Divine.

Existence

Being; the fundamental Reality; the indefinable, infinite, timeless, spaceless pure absolute.

Force

The power of being in motion; self-power of consciousness in a state of energy and activity; Shakti. The divine Force is the Divine itself in the body, of its power; in the individual it is a Force for illumination, transformation, purification.

Genius

Intuitive perception of Truth, superior and noble discernment; a fullness of inspiration of speech, creativity; revelation. (True genius is not yet fully developed in man)

gunas

The three primal qualities or modes of Nature; together they form the nature of things. The three gunas are:

* *sattwa* – the principle of assimilation, equilibrium and harmony;

* *rajas* – the principle of kinesis, passion, endeavour, struggle, initiation;

* *tamas* – the quality that hides or darkens; inertia.

Guru

Spiritual teacher; guide in spiritual life.

Integral Yoga

A union (yoga) with the Divine in all the parts of our being. This yoga implies not only the realisation of God but the entire consecration of the inner and outer life till it is fit to manifest a divine consciousness. In ordinary Yoga one main power of being or one group of its powers is made the means, vehicle, path. In a synthetic [integral] Yoga all powers are combined and included in the transmuting instrumentation; it is that which, having found the transcendent, can return upon the universe and possess it, retaining the power to freely descend as well as ascend the great stair of existence.

Ishwara

Lord; Master; God as the lord of Nature; also transcendent and individual.

Karma Yoga

The Yoga of works.

Karma

Action entailing its consequences.

Light

Light is not knowledge but the illumination that comes from above and liberates the being from obscurity and darkness; our sense by its incapacity has invented darkness. In truth there is nothing but Light, only it is a power of light either above or below our poor human vision's limited range.

Manas

The sense-mind; the sixth sense of classical Indian psychology in which all the others are gathered up.

Mind

The part of the nature which has to do with cognition and intelligence, with ideas, with mental perceptions etc. It is a consciousness which measures, limits, cuts out forms of things from the indivisible whole and contains them as if each were a separate integer. The Mind can be divided into five specific functions or levels: physical, vital, mental, psychic and spiritual. It is the mixture, of especially the first three that man usually identifies as *mind*, but modern psychology and experience demand a more lucid and exact appreciation.

Peace

A deep quietude where no disturbance can come – a quietude with a sense of established security and release. Peace as understood [in the Integral Yoga] is dynamic not passive. It is the foundation of purity.

Prakriti

Nature; nature-Force; creative energy.

Prana

The life-force; vital force; the breath.

Psychic being, the

The evolving soul of the individual, the divine portion in him which evolves from life to life, growing by its experiences until it becomes a fully conscious being. From its place behind the heart-centre, the psychic being supports the life, mind and body, aiding their growth and development. The term "soul" is often used as a synonym for "psychic being", but strictly speaking there is a distinction: the soul is the psychic essence; the psychic being is the soul-personality put forward and developed by the psychic essence to represent it in the evolution.

Purna Yoga

Integral Yoga, a union in all the parts of our being with the Divine and a consequent transmutation of all their now jarring elements into the harmony of a higher divine consciousness and existence. See also **Integral Yoga**

Glossary

Purusha

The true being or at least, in whatever plane it manifests, that which represents the true being; the witness which can become the master of the nature.

rasa

Sap or essence or taste of a thing

Reality

An infinite existence, an infinite consciousness, an infinite force and will, an infinite delight of being is the reality secret behind the appearances of the universe.

Sadhana

Spiritual practice; yogic discipline.

Sachchidananda

The one Divine Being with a triple aspect; the three indivisible aspects of the Supreme are:

* **Sat** – Being, Existence;
* **Chit** – Consciousness-Force;
* **Ananda** –Bliss, delight.

Self

The self-existent being,. The Self is being, not a being; it is the conscious essential existence, one in all.

Sense

The contact of mind with its objects creates what we call sense.

Shakti

The self-existent, self-cognitive, self-effective Power of the Lord, which expresses itself in the workings of Prakriti.

Spirit

The Consciousness above mind; the Atman or Self, which

is always in oneness with the Divine.

Supermind (the Supramental)

The Truth-Consciousness; the Truth in possession of itself and fulfilling itself by its own power. Its fundamental character is knowledge by identity, by that the Self is known ... but also the truth of manifestation is known.

Transitional being

Man is a transitional being, he is not final; for in him and high beyond him ascend the radiant degrees which climb to a divine supermanhood. The step from man towards superman is the next approaching achievement in the earth's evolution.

Truth-Consciousness

The Supermind. The Truth-Consciousness is the supramental state of consciousness which is a state of Oneness in which Truth arises from within. Below this is the Overmind consciousness where the dualities of Ishwara-Shakti and Purusha-Prakriti are established.

Understanding, the

The faculty which at once perceives, judges and discriminates; the true reason of the human being not subservient to the senses, to desire or to the blind force of habit, but working in its own right for mastery, for knowledge.

Unknowable, the

Not absolutely unknowable, but beyond mental knowledge, – can only be a higher degree in the intensity of being of that Something, a degree beyond the loftiest summit attainable by mental beings; an Absolute which can be so known that all truths can stand in it and find there their reconciliation.

Glossary

Upanishads, the

A class of philosophical writings attached to the Brahmanas giving an exposition of the secret meaning of the Veda and considered as the source of the Vedanta philosophy; the supreme ancient authority for the truths of the higher experience.

Yoga

From the Sanskrit *yug,* literally: joining; union; union with the Divine and the conscious seeking for this union; the discipline by which one enters through an awakening into an inner and higher consciousness; the spiritual practice leading to union; the art of conscious self-finding. To be one with the Eternal is the object of Yoga; there is no other object.

Yogi

Spiritual sage; mystic; one who practises yoga, but especially one who has attained the goal of yoga and is stabilised in spiritual realisation.

REFERENCES

REFERENCES

The texts in this Compilation are selected from the following editions of the works of Sri Aurobindo and The Mother:

SRI AUROBINDO BIRTH CENTENARY LIBRARY (SABCL) 1972

Volume	Title
5	*Collected Poems*
17	*The Hour of God*
18	*The Life Divine*, Book One and Book Two, Part One
19	*The Life Divine*, Book Two, Part Two
22	*Letters on Yoga*, Part One
23	*Letters on Yoga*, Part Two and Three
24	*Letters on Yoga*, Part Four

THE COMPLETE WORKS OF SRI AUROBINDO (CWSA) – 1997

Volume	Title
12	*Essays Divine and Human*
23	*The Synthesis of Yoga I*
24	*The Synthesis of Yoga II*
25	*The Human Cycle, The Ideal of Human Unity and War and Self-Determination*

27	*Letters on Poetry and Art*
33	*Savitri*, Part One
34	*Savitri*, Part Two

SEPARATE IMPRESSIONS OF SRI AUROBINDO'S WORKS

The Upanishads, Texts, Translations and Commentaries (UP) 2nd edition, 1981 – Seventh impression 2000

The Supramental Manifestation upon Earth (SM) 2nd edition, 1973 – Fifth impression 1995

Bulletin of Sri Aurobindo International Centre of Education (BULL)

All India Magazine (AIM)

COLLECTED WORKS OF THE MOTHER First Edition (CWM) 1978

Volume	Title
6	*Questions and Answers 1954*
7	*Questions and Answers 1955*
8	*Questions and Answers 1956*
9	*Questions and Answers 1957-58*
12	*On Education*

Each reference is preceded by the number (**in bold**) affixed at the end of each text, then its abbreviated form which includes the name of the author and edition, followed by the volume number and page number. For example: **1.** SABCL 5:165, which is the reference of Sri Aurobindo's poem *Our godhead calls us*.

The references follow:

References

1. SABCL 5:165
2. BULL 15 Aug. 1977:10-12
3. SABCL 19:684
4. Ibid., 5:164
5. Ibid., 19:694-95
6. BULL 15 Aug.1977:12
7. Ibid., :14-16
8. SABCL 18:162-63
9. Ibid., 18:235-36
10. SM 81-83
11. UP 224
12. SABCL 22:322-23
13. Ibid., 5:132
14. Ibid., 5:137
15. Ibid., 18:46-47
16. UP 192-93
17. SABCL 5:133
18. Ibid., 5:163
19. Ibid., 5:145
20. UP 144-45
21. SABCL 18:62-63
22. CWSA 19:565-67
23. SABCL 18:210-11
24. SM 77-78
25. UP 178-79
26. Ibid., 179
27. SABCL 5:157
28. UP 133-34
29. SABCL 18:118-19
30. Ibid., 23:686
31. Ibid., 5:163
32. CWM 6:316-17
33. CWSA 23:75-76
34. SABCL 22:327
35. Ibid., 18:413-14
36. Ibid., 19:772-73
37. Ibid., 19:717-18
38. Ibid., 24:1256
39. Ibid., 22:330
40. Ibid., 19:649
41. Ibid., 23:705
42. Ibid., 22:330-31
43. Ibid., 22:331
44. Ibid., 24:1270
45. Ibid., 24:1270
46. Ibid., 18:537-38
47. Ibid.,18:562
48. CWSA 24:646-47
49. SABCL 18:62
50. CWSA 24:651
51. Ibid., 23:314
52. Ibid., 23:351
53. SABCL 22:334
54. Ibid., 22:336
55. Ibid., 22:336-37
56. Ibid., 5:95
57. Ibid., 22:334
58. Ibid., 24:1108
59. Ibid., 22:341
60. Ibid., 22:326-27
61. CWSA 23:351
62. Ibid., 24:659-660
63. SABCL 22:340-41
64. Ibid., 5:99-100
65. Ibid., 18:414
66. CWSA 23:354-55
67. SABCL 18:607-11
68. CWSA 23:305-06
69. SABCL 19:718-19
70. CWSA 23:352-53
71. SABCL 19:719
72. Ibid., 5:103
73. Ibid., 22:320-21
74. CWSA 23:351-52
75. Ibid., 24:664-65
76. Ibid., 24:667

77. Ibid., 23:310-11
78. SABCL 24:1251
79. Ibid., 18:526-27
80. Ibid., 24:1321-22
81. CWSA 24:667
82. Ibid., 23:295
83. Ibid., 23:303-04
84. Ibid., 33:284-85
85. Ibid., 23:330-31
86. Ibid., 33:285-86
87. Ibid., 23:370-71
88. Ibid., 23:24
89. Ibid., 23:283-84
90. Ibid.,23:316
91. CWM 6:328-29
92. SABCL 24:1252
93. Ibid., 24:1252-53
94. Ibid., 24:1254
95. CWSA 33:286-87
96. Ibid., 33:134-35
97. Ibid., 23:375
98. Ibid., 23:372-73
99. SABCL 22:75-76
100. Ibid., 22:292
101. Ibid., 22:325
102. Ibid., 22:324
103. Ibid., 24:1111-12
104. Ibid., 24:1197-98
105. AIM Oct. 1977 6-7
106. SABCL 22:295-96
107. Ibid., 22:283
108. Ibid., 22:301
109. Ibid., 18:226
110. Ibid., 18:225
111. Ibid., 23:308-09
112. Ibid., 22:309
113. CWM 4:26-27
114. CWSA 25:33
115. Ibid., 23:138-39
116. SABCL 24:1647-48
117. CWSA 23:337-38
118. SABCL 19:854-55
119. CWSA 23:69-70
120. SABCL 23:946
121. CWM 7:41
122. SABCL 22:324-25
123. Ibid., 22:325
124. Ibid., 19:882
125. Ibid., 19:857
126. CWM 9:418-21
127. SABCL 19:856
128. Ibid., 19:722
129. CWSA 23:29
130. SABCL 18:318
131. CWSA 24:792-93
132. SABCL 18:227-28
133. Ibid., 18:228-29
134. CWSA 23:26
135. SABCL 19:902
136. Ibid., 18:276-77
137. CWSA 33:256-57
138. Ibid., 23:148
139. SABCL 17:31
140. Ibid., 5:129
141. BULL 24 Apr. 1977:12-14
142. SABCL 18:274-75
143. Ibid., 22:278
144. Ibid., 22:282
145. Ibid., 22:283
146. Ibid., 22:299
147. UP 43
148. SABCL 22:283
149. Ibid., 22:282
150. Ibid.,22:277
151. Ibid., 22:276
152. Ibid., 18:275-76

References

153. Ibid., 23:1022
154. CWSA 27:21-22
155. SABCL 19:939-40
156. CWSA 23:79-80
157. SABCL 19:940-41
158. CWSA 24:825-26
159. SABCL 19:944-46
160. CWSA 27:23
161. Ibid., 23:477-78
162. Ibid., 24:809
163. Ibid., 24:806-08
164. Ibid., 24:811
165. Ibid., 24:898-99
166. Ibid., 27:60-62
167. SABCL 18:278-280
168. CWSA 23:415
169. SABCL 5:151
170. Ibid., 23:1085
171. Ibid., 23:1084
172. Ibid., 23:1085
173. Ibid., 18:237-38
174. Ibid., 18:234-35
175. Ibid., 19:845-46
176. Ibid., 17:22
177. CWSA 23:183-84
178. CWM 8:344-46
179. SM 61-62
180. SABCL 5:161
181. SM 95-96
182. Ibid., 108
183. Ibid., 59-60
184. CWSA 33:343-44
185. Ibid., 23:297-98
186. Ibid., 12: 150-51
187. CWM 12: 187-88